NO MORE CRUMBS

NO MORE CRUMBS

Your Invitation to
Sit & Feast at the King's Table

Rod Parsley

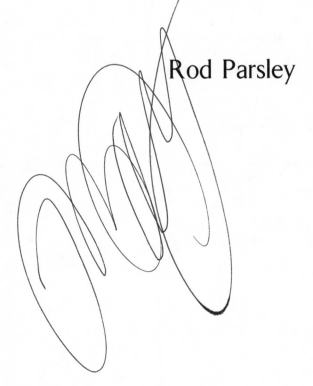

Creation House
Strang Communications Company
600 Rinehart Road
Lake Mary, Florida 32746
Web site: http://www.creationhouse.com

Unless otherwise noted, all Scripture quotations are from
the King James Version of the Bible.

Scripture quotations marked *The Message* are from THE MESSAGE.
Copyright © 1993, 1994, 1995. Used by permission of
NavPress Publishing Group.

Library of Congress Cataloging-in-Publication Data:
Parsley, Rod.
    No more crumbs / Rod Parsley.
        p.   cm.
    1. Success—Religious aspects—Christianity.   2. Christian life.
    3. Success—Biblical teaching.   4. Bible—Biography.   I. Title.
BV4598.3.P37   1997   97-36037
248.4—dc21   CIP
Printed in the United States of America
7890123 BVG 765432

To My Loving Wife, Joni Parsley

PROVERBS 18:22 SAYS, "Whoso findeth a wife findeth a good thing, and obtaineth favour of the Lord."

Nearly twenty years ago I had the privilege of being introduced to you, my lovely wife, Joni—a wonderful woman whom God had hewn out of a rock just for me. I will never forget that before we were married we dated for seven years, which our pastor, Dr. Lester Sumrall, so affectionately termed as the Tribulation Period. Several months before we were engaged Dr. Sumrall looked at me and said, "When are you going to marry that girl?"

In a time when marriage is fast becoming a relic of the past and commitment is a crumbling value at best, I have been blessed that our marriage has truly been made in heaven. God has sovereignly joined us together, and on our wedding day I can honestly say that I married my best friend.

Time and eternity are not long enough to tell you of my

deep love, admiration, and respect for you. We have been blessed to have two wonderful children, Ashton and Austin, to whom you have ceaselessly devoted your time and love. You are an outstanding mother whose personal relationship with God has shown our children our unfailing love for them as well as the inexhaustible love of their heavenly Father.

Joni, you are also a woman of tremendous honor and character whose life exemplifies unwavering faith, immovable courage, and endless perseverance. You are a constant source of strength, peace, and support to my life. Even in our most tragic moments, such as the loss of our unborn child, you have stood valiantly and victoriously in the face of discouragement and defeat.

Throughout my life I have never met a more godly woman. You are one of the greatest Christians I know, and I am so proud to be your husband.

It is for these reasons that this book is lovingly dedicated to you, Joni—my beautiful wife, a wonderful mother, and my best friend.

Joni, thank you for standing by my side and being an encouragement in the good times and a comfort in the bad times. You are the greatest gift from God I could have ever hoped for, and I cannot imagine life without you. You are my joy and happiness in this world, and I love you with all of my heart.

Contents

Introduction

Surviving on the Crumbs

IMAGINE THAT you could strap yourself into a time machine and travel a thousand years into the past. Unseen by those whom you visited, you could travel to faraway lands and see the stories within the stories written in the ancient texts of Scripture.

Where would you choose to go? Perhaps you might dare to visit Galilee during the reign of Caesar Augustus and watch as no movie could ever depict the real life and drama of a prophet from Nazareth named Jesus. Or you might travel to a place much more distant in time in order to watch Moses lead slaves from Goshen across the Red Sea as they begin a forty-year trek through the wilderness. Or if you could endure the pain—and I cannot imagine any of us could—you would hover in space above a hill called Golgotha, the Place of the Skull. There you would witness the most dramatic moment in all history, when the King of Glory suffered and died on a cross for your sins.

Let me take you back to some lesser-known scenes. While their details are less familiar, their lessons will dramatically change your life. Settle back. Strap yourself in. This ride will be much more profitable and inspiring than any circus or amusement-park ride. You will peer into the past and see mirrored in the lives of the ancients your own story . . . and a vision of your future that far surpasses anything you could have hoped for or imagined.

SITE 1: LO-DEBAR (CA. 990 B.C.)

FIRST, YOUR TIME MACHINE darts across a desolate desert and comes to rest over a tiny village east of Jordan in the middle of nowhere. The town is Lo-debar. So deserted are its streets and impoverished its huts that you wonder if anyone of any significance could live there, except for a few pilgrims who might spend a night there to rest on their way to some-place else—anyplace else!

Outside a small mud hut on the periphery of the isolated cluster of huts, you spy a crippled young man who is baking a meager cake of grain in a small earthen oven. Rags cover his body and a pair of crutches lay close by his side. His face is streaked with soot, and he doesn't appear to have bathed or shaven in months.

Curiously, you notice a caravan is approaching over the horizon, purposely heading toward this outpost in no man's land. Lo-debar—what a depressing and God-forsaken place! No one would voluntarily choose to live there. So why is this young man stuck in this desolate village? Does his physical handicap keep him in Lo-debar, or might some spiritual bondage force him to seek a lonely, self-imposed exile? Has he run away from something or someone in the past whom he fears?

As your time machine pulls away from the town, you notice the caravan is drawing ever closer. A banner that flies from the lead mount is bordered in royal purple with the insignia of a lion. What important, royal entourage could this be? And why is it headed toward such an insignificant destination?

SITE 2: MOUNT CARMEL (CA. 860 B.C.)

AS YOU APPROACH Mount Carmel in northern Israel, you stare breathlessly at a massive gathering of Israelites, swarming together like ants completely covering a hill. A huge altar is built at the top of the mountain, and hundreds of priests are dancing around it, chanting in loud voices to imaginary deities.

Off to the side, a royal throne covered by a silk canopy is occupied by a bearded king, who has eyes more evil than anyone you have ever seen. He looks intently back and forth upon the dancing priests and then glances up to the heavens, as if he expects something to happen above the mountain in response to the antics of the pagan prophets below.

Around Mount Carmel, the plains which are usually fertile are barren and dusty. The parched land doesn't appear to have seen rain for many years. Off to the side of the dancing priests stands a solitary figure with a long beard and blazing eyes. He seems bemused by the gyrations of the cultists.

So what is the meaning of this gathering? And when will sowers in the barren valley once again produce a harvest? What will the fate of these pagans be? And who is the solitary figure who, though isolated from the crowd, might well be the main actor in this unfolding drama?

SITE 3: A PIG'S STY (DATE UNKNOWN)

AS YOUR TIME MACHINE continues to drift across the arid desert and through the cloudless sky, you notice a pig farm stretching for acres along the Euphrates River. The stench nauseates you, even though you are miles above the land. You pity the workers who must daily wade through the filthy pens slopping food for the hogs.

Then a broken and dejected young man catches your eye. He seems unaccustomed to his environment. As you draw closer, you notice an odd action on his part. He seems to be examining every eaten corn husk that he is cleaning out of the pens.

What is he doing? You are repulsed when you finally realize that he is actually feeding himself the uneaten kernels on each husk that has already been gnawed on by the hogs.

Then you notice that the features of this young man are definitely Semitic—he is undoubtedly a Hebrew. Why is a

Jewish man working in such a ceremonially unclean place? Surely he knows that all pigs are unclean. He must be a slave. But how did he end up in Mesopotamia tending hogs for Gentiles? What tragedy brought him here? Is there any way out for him?

SITE 4: THE SEA OF GALILEE (CA. 29 A.D.)

AS YOU TRAVEL forward in time, you recognize the Sea of Galilee. On its northern shore you notice the bustling town of Capernaum. Fishing boats litter the seashore and dot the sparkling waters of the lake around which Jesus ministered. You strain your eyes to see Jesus walking the streets of the city. Then at last you catch a glimpse of a small band of men walking toward the synagogue. In the middle of the group is a bronzed man who walks briskly, with an air of authority. *That must be Jesus!* you think, as your heart begins to pound.

As Jesus enters the synagogue, you notice a frail man carefully cradling a withered hand enter behind the group. A crowd begins to gather outside the synagogue, as not everyone who has come can fit inside the building. It must be the Sabbath, and Jesus is going to worship. Will He say anything or simply sit there quietly? Is the crowd gathering because He is there? Will He notice the man with the crippled hand?

DRIFTING SOUTH over the Sea of Galilee, you pass over the east bank village of Hippus. It's now dusk, and everyone in

5

the village seems to be at rest on the Sabbath—everyone, that is, but a woman who is secretly sneaking out of the village toward the town's well.

Something strange catches your eye. Behind the woman trails a thin, crimson line wherever she goes. Is it blood? Who dares to do work by going to the well on the Sabbath? Could she be secretly going there because no one else would be out in the streets? Why is she bleeding? What has happened in her life to bring her to such a state of fear and secrecy?

WHAT SEASON OF LIFE ARE YOU IN?

IN MY EARLIER BOOK, *No Dry Season*, I shared the truths of how God by His Spirit is bringing into our lives a new season of renewal, refreshing, restoration, and revival. We are coming out of the desert of spiritual poverty and into a fresh move of God's Spirit for this final generation of standard bearers.

> As Christians, we do not have to barely make it through life.

Now it is time to consider how we can feast at His table in the midst of His abundance and blessing. Leaving our dry seasons behind, we need a breakthrough of massive proportions in order to claim the limitless inheritance given us by our King. As Christians, we do not have to barely make it through life.

Some are simply holding on until the rapture. Destitute and desperate, they scratch out a meager existence in the Lo-debar of their lives, never taking their rightful places at the King's table.

You may be emerging from your dry season but still not claiming your inheritance in Christ Jesus. Instead of feasting at His banquet table, you are abandoned in Lo-debar; waiting on Mount Carmel for God to send down the fire into your life; gnawing on leftovers in the pig sty where you've been living; or carrying some paralyzing burden or affliction that causes you to be overwhelmed with shame and guilt. Instead of attacking the enemy and possessing the Promised Land that God has provided, you have allowed the giants of fear, unbelief, complacency, discouragement and the opinions of others, to rob you of your future.

This book is for you—the outcast, the stranger, and the alien to the promises of God. In these pages you will discover:

- Your *peace* and reconciliation with God under the new covenant of Christ.

- Your *position* of royalty that God has restored for you.

- Your *provision* from God to renew your attack on the enemy and claim victory through Christ.

- Your *perpetual privilege* to reap a *promised harvest* and experience a dramatic breakthrough in your finances, health, family, and ministry.

7

Now journey with me through the pages of biblical history and discover the truths that will empower you to declare with power and authority for your life and your family:

No More Crumbs!

1

~∞~

A Place Called Lo-debar

THE STOOPED, AGED SERVANT shuffled reluctantly toward the small opening of the solitary, diminutive mud hut—the smallest one of the desolate, God-forsaken village of Lo-debar. He resented his assignment.

Once, Ziba thought, *I served the Lord's anointed, King Saul. Now I am seeking a crippled reject.*

Years ago Ziba's life had been filled with significant tasks that honored the king and brought favors and special privileges his way. He had ushered important diplomats from distant empires into the king's presence. Those seeking an audience with the king would often seek out Ziba, bribing him with spices and scarce fruits in order to have just one moment with the king.

But for many years now, King Saul and his beloved son, Jonathan, had been dead. Since their demise, Saul's faithful servant had quietly lived in the capital of the new king, David ben Jesse. Ziba paused in his approach to the hut as he reminisced over glory days from the past. Like a desert mirage forming in the distant haze, Ziba's memories played scenes from the early years of Saul's reign.

DURING SAUL'S MONARCHY, David, the shepherd boy turned king, had defeated King Saul's enemies and smashed the Philistines in the Valley of Elah when a single stone flung from his sling penetrated the forehead of giant Goliath, killing him instantly. Ziba smiled to himself. What a magnificent victory that had been! David cut off Goliath's head, and the armies of Israel slayed hundreds of Philistines until sunset!

For a time, David was Saul's mighty warrior. But when the news of David's victory spread throughout the kingdom, the young women began to applaud and praise him with the proclamation, "Saul has slain his thousands but David his ten thousands." With this torrent of tribute, Saul became more and more jealous. Evil spirits began to haunt the king, increasingly robbing his days of sanity and plunging him into desperate fits of depression and rage.

Not only a fearless soldier, David was also an accomplished musician, often playing spiritual psalms on his lyre as he sang in a soothing baritone to calm the agitated Saul. For fleeting moments, Saul would experience a sense of peace before falling again into the abyss of his dark side.

These demonic forces, only briefly subsiding with the songs of the shepherd boy, began to muster legions of jealous and wrathful spirits to work through Saul against David. Consumed with hate, Saul first tried to kill David and then fitfully abandoned all affairs of state to pursue the shepherd turned hero. David became an outlaw who spent his days hiding in the wilderness and fleeing for his life.

For years the king pursued David with a vengeance. Saul's obsession with hunting him down left Israel's enemies unchallenged. When they realized King Saul was preoccupied with his search for David, the Philistines rebuilt their armies and rekindled countless attacks against Israel. Abandoning his fledgling nation, King Saul no longer kept the Philistines at bay, but instead, chased every rumor about David's whereabouts, hoping to corner him and rid himself of this rival whom the people loved more than their possessed and sometimes insane king.

Too late, Saul turned his attention to the invading Philistines. Demented and tormented by demons, he sought the psychic counsel of a witch at Endor, hoping to get one last prophetic word from the spirit of Samuel. To Saul's chagrin, the only word he heard prophesied his imminent defeat and death.

On Mount Gilboa, King Saul and Jonathan fought to the death as the Philistines routed Israel's overmatched and underequipped army. For a brief time, Saul's son, Ishbosheth had ruled part of Israel. But David's mighty warrior, Joab, had first killed Ishbosheth's general, Abner, and then Joab's men had murdered Ishbosheth. Fleeing before Joab's mighty men, all those loyal to Saul who sought escape were slaughtered. All

11

died by the sword, except one child named Mephibosheth, which means "shameful one." During the confusion and panic of fleeing from Joab's men, young Mephibosheth's nurse dropped him. The nurse managed to escape with Mephibosheth to Lo-debar of Manasseh in Gilead across the Jordan, but the tumble permanently crippled the child. Even though he was Jonathan's son and the grandson of King Saul, Mephibosheth was destined to grow up in obscurity—crippled physically, emotionally, and spiritually.

> Mephibosheth was destined to grow up in obscurity—crippled physically, emotionally, and spiritually.

ZIBA RELUCTANTLY made his way toward Mephibosheth's hut. Consumed by the emotions of painful memories, he paused once more before pushing aside the woolen flap that half-covered the small opening which served as the hut's only entry and exit. He winced, remembering the fear that had shaken him as he had faced King David. There he had learned about a stirring within the king's heart that would forever change Ziba's destiny and the future of the lame boy he would now meet for the first time.

JUST DAYS BEFORE in the Jerusalem palace, King David startled everyone with the disturbing question, "Is there yet any who is left of the house of Saul, that I may show him kindness for Jonathan's sake?"

After David's coronation as the King of Israel, Ziba had quietly settled on the outskirts of Jerusalem. With Saul and Jonathan dead, Ziba's only future had been an impoverished and lonely existence. He had always secretly admired the shepherd boy who had slain lions, bears, giants, and Philistines before he had finally risen to the throne of Israel. Yet, Ziba knew that should his past loyalty to Saul ever surface, his life might be endangered. The enemies of Saul were now in power, and Ziba was but an expendable relic from a former monarchy. All his former associates were dead. Ziba had simply hoped to live out his waning years in obscure peace, comforted only by his tears and past sorrows.

But someone in King David's palace discovered Ziba's residence, not far from Jerusalem's smoldering garbage heap in the Valley of Gehenna. That fateful day arrived when soldiers pounded on the door of his humble adobe hut and escorted him into the king's presence.

David had demanded, "Are you Ziba?"

Trembling with fright and falling on his face before the king, Ziba managed only to whisper, "I am your servant."

"Is there not yet any of the house of Saul, that I may show the kindness of God unto him?" asked David.

With regal authority and expectation, King David's question, like the sword he had used to cut off Goliath's head, pierced quickly into Ziba's mind. The king was seeking a long forgotten orphan, whose memory had almost been completely repressed by Ziba.

Ziba's soul suddenly flooded with past sorrows, present fears, and complete bewilderment. Why, after so many years, was David interested in any of Saul's descendants who might have survived? Was this a cruel trick? Did David still harbor some unrequited anger against Saul that could only be mitigated by exterminating his last remaining seed? If Ziba revealed the truth, would he be instantly executed for having been Saul's faithful servant years ago? Or, could it be that David had some genuine compassion for Saul's only living descendant?

UNKNOWN TO ZIBA, David had spent many restless nights reliving his grief over his best friend's death. Secretly, years before, David and Saul's son Jonathan had entered into a blood covenant as brothers bound eternally together—heart to heart. Both had sworn to love and protect one another and one another's family for as long as each should live. Then Jonathan, David's beloved friend, had been killed in battle. Though reports had assured David that all of Saul's family and loyalists had been slain, still a rumor persisted that one of Jonathan's sons had escaped across the Jordan.

For years, David had employed agents to track down any

clues to the whereabouts of this last surviving descendant of Jonathan. Finally, sources had revealed that an aging servant from Saul's court was living on the outskirts of Jerusalem. David's heart raced with hope and anticipation as he sent soldiers to bring this servant, Ziba, to him. Ziba was David's best and last hope of uncovering the truth to any rumor about a surviving son of Jonathan.

> # David knew in his heart that if any of Jonathan's household survived, he would fulfill his vow to Jonathan.

David knew in his heart that if any of Jonathan's household survived, he would fulfill his vow to Jonathan. That survivor would be treated like his own son and given a place of honor in the kingdom. That was the only way left this side of the grave for David to show his love for Jonathan and keep his covenant. So now David looked upon this prostrated and trembling servant of Saul, anxiously awaiting his reply.

BEFORE ANY PEACE could settle his spirit, Ziba's mouth blurted out the secret: "There is still a son of Jonathan, who is lame in his feet."

David's face filled with surprise and then relief. Rising slowly from his throne, the king approached the shaking and frightened Ziba, hopefully whispering, "Where is he?" David grabbed Ziba by the robe and stood him on his feet. Face-to-face, the weathered countenance and terrified eyes of an old man looked directly into the bronze, handsome face and dark, penetrating eyes of the king. With his heart in his throat and still shaking uncontrollably, Ziba replied, "Behold, he is in the house of Machir the son of Ammiel, in Lo-debar."

Immediately, David ordered Ziba to guide two men from his royal guard and rush quickly to Lo-debar. There he was to find Jonathan's son and return with him to David's palace. The journey from Jerusalem, down through the wilderness into Jericho and across the Jordan, had been rushed and rugged in the sweltering heat of the blazing, desert sun. They had not stopped for sleep as they pushed through the night and stopped only briefly for bread and water. Making in two days a journey of what normally took three by foot, they had arrived at Lo-debar and now stood in front of Mephibosheth's crumbling hut.

COVERED WITH SWEAT, aching with fatigue, and trembling with anticipation, Ziba pulled back the ragged, wool sheepskin covering the entry to the orphan's hut. As he stepped inside, his waning eyesight could not immediately adjust from the brilliant sunlight to the dark shadows of the musty, one room hut. As the shadows slowly formed into recognizable shapes, Ziba squinted to make out the detail of the hut's interior.

Reluctantly the shadows unveiled their secrets, and the

sparsely furnished room came into view. A solitary ray of light penetrated a small opening in the hut's roof, through which smoke escaped from smoldering coals under a small earthen oven in the center of the room. Pungent odors from soiled rags and unwashed pots filled Ziba's nostrils, causing him to choke and cough. Everything in the hut smelled rank and decayed. He turned his head and surveyed the room, to discover only a small table, a stool, a few clay pots, and a small urn of oil occupied the space. What appeared to be a heap of dirty rags was piled on a straw mat off to his right side. Beside the rags were two rough-hewn sticks the length of a man's arm, each wrapped on one end with strips of cloth.

As Ziba began to cough uncontrollably from the smoke and irritating odors, the pile of rags on the straw mat began to move. Tears formed in Ziba's eyes as they smarted from the smoke. Nonetheless, through puffy, reddened eyes, Ziba noticed that a frail figure covered with rags began to stir. A skeleton with skin hanging loosely from it struggled to stand by using the two sticks as crutches.

Like ghosts from each other's pasts, the old man and the orphaned boy stared at each other for a minute that seemed like eternity. Mephibosheth's gaunt face with its dark sockets for eyes fixed a glassy stare upon his intruder. His eyes no longer reflected the fear and desperate loneliness of wondering when he might be discovered and killed as a relative of the disgraced, dead King Saul. They were simply glazed with the hopelessness that reaches far beyond poverty and hunger into the bottomless abyss of one who no longer lives, but merely exists.

A SENTENCE of living death had been pronounced over Mephibosheth years before the moment he met Ziba by the accuser and author of death, the father of lies, the archenemy of the anointed, whose name is variously given as Satan or Lucifer. For years, that hut had been a living tomb, and its inhabitant dwelled in bondage to a tragic past and an unbroken curse.

Mephibosheth had not claimed his inheritance as royalty. He was the descendant of the anointed one of Israel, yet he exchanged the truth of his position for the lie of his circumstance. He had come to believe that his present had to be chained to past failures and tragedies. The anointing on his life had not been originally earned by his father, Jonathan, or his grandfather, Saul. Anointing to royalty can never be earned: it is always imparted as a gift. And what has been given can never be removed by any circumstance or person other than the One who gave the anointing. Not even King David could harm a descendant of someone who had been specially anointed by

Anointing to royalty can never be earned: it is always imparted as a gift.

God. Years before, when presented with the opportunity to kill King Saul, the outlaw David confessed, "I will not put forth mine hand against my lord [King Saul]; for he is the Lord's anointed" (1 Sam. 24:10).

Now the aged servant Ziba stood face-to-face with deposed and dejected royalty, Mephibosheth.

As a fog that slowly lifts over a miry bog, Mephibosheth's glazed stare transformed into pained recognition. "Has an old man, servant to my dead grandfather, come to kick the last surviving dog of Saul's seed?" he scornfully asked.

Ziba almost spoke a rebuke, but then bit his tongue. No matter what he thought or how downcast this orphan appeared to be, his position was unchanged. Ziba was still the servant, and Mephibosheth was still royalty.

"My lord," Ziba respectfully replied with a bowed head, "King David requests the honor of your presence in his court."

"How so after all these years?" Mephibosheth asked with unbelief. "Does he now wish to further disgrace the last of Saul's family? Am I to be mocked, tortured, and then killed before all those of David's court? Can he not let me simply lie here and die? I am worth nothing to him. I deserve nothing from him, not even the stale crumbs falling from his table that the dogs will not eat."

"You must come, my lord. It is the command of the king." And with that, Ziba motioned to the soldiers, who entered the hut and carried Mephibosheth out of his desolate dwelling place and set him upon the king's royal mount for the ride back to Jerusalem.

OUT OF LO-DEBAR rode the King's entourage. Lo-debar! The very name of that place means "not a pasture." Lo-debar was the dwelling place of lack, poverty, dryness, and desolation. It was the wilderness, desert, and empty field of no sowing and no harvest.

Lo-debar—nothing was there. Never intended to be a destination or a dwelling place, Lo-debar had become Mephibosheth's prison of emptiness and isolation. It was his hell of existence—not life, but a living death.

THERE WAS ONLY ONE WAY out of Lo-debar. The only way out required that a prior promise be remembered and a cherished covenant be fulfilled.

When in Lo-debar, it seems that existing on stale crumbs is the only option. Lo-debar's residents are tempted to believe the lie that there is nothing beyond its boundaries. For Mephibosheth, Lo-debar seemed like the end of the journey, the final chapter in a tragic existence. Lame and alone, the king's descendant appeared doomed to an existence devoid of hope or harvest. He may have been born royalty, but he would die an outcast. Or would he? Against all hope, overcoming every circumstance, and beyond Mephibosheth's wildest dreams, the impossible was happening. He was riding out of Lo-debar and from that moment on, there would be:

No More Crumbs!

2

By Invitation Only

T REMBLING WITH FEAR, Mephibosheth entered into King David's palace. Eyes that had grown accustomed to seeing lack, poverty, and emptiness were now filled with the splendors of the king's power and wealth. He could not imagine himself having so much after existing on so little. *Kings may live in great abundance*, he thought, *but I will never amount to anything but a castoff reject whose only claim to fame is a dead, disgraced grandfather who once was a king*. Mephibosheth had resigned himself to mere existence sustained by crumbs—and no more!

To his surprise, Mephibosheth was not taken immediately to the formal throne room. Rather, Ziba led him into a small chamber where a hot bath had been prepared by servants. Next to the bronze bathing tub were a new robe of white linen and sandals crafted from expensive leather.

"Clean yourself, put on the robe and sandals, and prepare yourself to dine with the king," Ziba curtly commanded and then quickly exited the room.

Setting aside his crutches, Mephibosheth carefully balanced himself against the side of the tub and tore away the rotten rags from his body. For the first time in years, he smelled the stench of his filthy clothes and flesh. He recognized the odor of putrid flesh about to rot and fall off one who was malnourished and merely existing, with death just around the corner. Carefully lifting his feeble legs over the side of the tub, he slowly eased himself down into the fragrant, warm water of his first bath in years.

Closing his eyes, Mephibosheth soaked in the first luxury he had ever known. He began to dream of something better. *What if I were king? What if things were different? What would I do to David if our situations were reversed?*

His thoughts were rudely interrupted by an impatient voice outside his door. "Hurry," scolded Ziba. "King David has now arrived in the palace and is making his way to the royal table. You must dress and come with me in just a few moments."

Startled back to reality, Mephibosheth quickly finished bathing and lifted himself out of the tub. Steadying himself with one arm and drying with the other, he rushed to ready himself for the most important encounter of his life. He carefully balanced himself on one crutch as he slipped the seamless robe over his head and tied a purple sash about his waist. *Purple is the color of royalty*, he remembered. He had only seen this color once on a faded cloth that had belonged to his father, Jonathan.

Grabbing his other crutch, Mephibosheth limped toward the hallway, where he found Ziba impatiently waiting for him. The two strangers, unknowingly about to become lifelong partners, made their way into the massive, royal dining room. The air was filled with tantalizing aromas of roasted lamb, tangy leeks and onions, and strong drink. At first, all Mephibosheth could do was stare at the overflowing banquet table. Never had he seen clusters of grapes and mounds of olives like this. Candles blazed to light the room. The finest pottery graced the table. Elaborate tapestries hung from the walls. And musicians played worshipful choruses. The strains of a few songs sounded familiar—like the ones his nurse often hummed during his childhood.

So caught up in the awesome surroundings, Mephibosheth had almost forgotten to look up toward the head of the table. Now trembling again almost to the point of falling, he fearfully looked up and saw a ruddy, bearded man coming toward him. His eyes sparkled with delight. His simple robe flowed with graceful ease. And strength seemed to bathe his bronze skin with an unearthly glow.

It's King David! Now I'm a dead man, Mephibosheth thought. *He will knock me down and kill me with a single blow like he did with all his other enemies.*

Before another thought had time to paralyze his brain, Mephibosheth found himself lifted up into the strong embrace of the king of Israel. David hugged Mephibosheth so hard that it seemed for a moment that every bone in the cripple's fragile body might break. David erupted into sobs and laughter. Dazed and stunned, Mephibosheth clung onto his father's friend and began to sob gently.

> # Mephibosheth had to move from Lo-debar to the palace in order to claim his blessing—and so do we!

"For years, I have sought any child born to my covenant brother, Jonathan. Now I have found you, Mephibosheth. You will eat at my table. You will have Ziba and other servants wait on you day and night. You will be dressed in the finest robes and have your every need supplied. No longer will you eat the crumbs left for dogs. You are royalty, and you will have a place at my table as long as you live. I will show you kindness for Jonathan's sake," declared King David.

ARE YOU SURPRISED that the greatest king in Israel's history—David son of Jesse—would be so magnanimous toward a helpless cripple? David's response to Mephibosheth closely parallels how God loves us. A covenant blessing awaited Mephibosheth that he never dreamed or even could hope for in his wildest imagination. Nonetheless, he had been born royalty and was pursued by King David until his rightful place at the king's table could be secured. While Mephibosheth had resigned himself to a life of scraps and crumbs, his true inheritance was rooted in a covenant blessing that promised an abundant life. Mephibosheth had to move from Lo-debar to the palace in order to claim his blessing—and so do we!

THE COVENANT PROMISE

DAVID HAD MADE more than a human promise to his beloved friend, Jonathan. He had cut a blood covenant before God with Jonathan. David is not simply being kind or generous to the child of an old buddy. He is honoring a timeless, eternal covenant sealed in blood and in the name of Almighty God, El Shaddai.

When a covenant was cut during biblical times, it represented a vow that could not be broken. Covenants are the most sacred promises ever made. So the blood covenant made between Jonathan and David not only bound them together as friends, but also bound their families together so that one family would take care of the other if a tragedy should strike.

In Hebrew, the word for covenant is *b^erit*, which comes from the verb meaning "to cut." It was common practice to set up a stone cut engraved with the words of the promise to mark the covenant (Gen. 31:54–55). Apart from blood ties, the covenant was the way in the ancient world that relation-ships were formed between nations and people. The relationship between Jonathan and David was a "covenant of the Lord" (1 Sam. 18:3; 20:8; 23:18) in which God Himself was the witness and surety of the covenant.

Why did David and Jonathan cut a covenant together? There are only three reasons for cutting a covenant:

1. *Protection*

A covenant may be cut between stronger and weaker parties for the sake of protection. The weaker person or group of people needs the protection of the stronger one; therefore, the two parties seal a covenant of mutual loyalty.

2. *Business*

This form of covenant is based on the simple business principle that the sum is greater than its parts. In other words, if I join my assets with yours then we will both eat the fruit of them. Together we will profit much more than in going our separate ways.

3. *Love*

Marriage is the highest expression of this form of covenant. When a man and a woman join together in the perfect union of marriage, they vow their perpetual fidelity, love, and honor to one another. Their two spirits become one, and they become a powerful spiritual force. One alone can put a thousand to flight, but a husband and wife together can drive away ten thousand.

The covenant between David and Jonathan is described in 1 Samuel 18. As part of the covenant ceremony, Jonathan gave David his robe, sword, and armor. He was indicating in covenant with David that everything he possessed, David now possessed and that his protection now covered David. By giving to David his armor and sword, Jonathan was cutting a covenant of protection with David that he would call upon the armies of Israel, if necessary, to protect him. In such ancient covenants, blood was also shed by each person cutting their right wrist and co-mingling the blood or dripping the blood into wine and drinking the "cup of the covenant" together. Jesus called upon this imagery when He gave us the "cup of the new covenant" of His blood shed for us in the Lord's Supper (Matt. 26:26–29; 1 Cor. 11:23–26).

This blood covenant of promise between Jonathan and David could not be annulled, set aside, or broken. It was a sacred trust, just like the marriage covenant between husband and wife. God intends that such a covenant not be broken.

Marriage exemplifies such a blood covenant of promise. I say to my wife, Joni, that everything I have belongs to her and vice versa. I will protect her with all the strength and life within me. I clothe her in the best garments. I buy her expensive jewelry. I want others to know that she is in covenant with me and has the best. She doesn't have the crumbs left over from my work: she sits at the banquet table of my love. My banner over her is love, and I give her all that I have. I am in covenant with my wife. I do not want her to wear clothes from the thrift store or to have to beg others for something she needs. Why?

All His provision and protection have been laid up as an inheritance for us, if we will only claim it.

Because her husband works hard, and God blesses us. We sow our seed into the good soil of His kingdom, and God multiplies our seed. I get joy out of giving to her because I am in covenant with her.

Likewise, God so loved the world that He gave us His only begotten Son (John 3:16). All His provision and protection have already been laid up as an inheritance for us, if we will only claim it. The same was true for Mephibosheth. Because of the covenant between his father and David, he had an inheritance of provision and protection laid up for him before his birth. Even though his grandfather, King Saul, attempted to kill David many times, David refused to touch "God's anointed" king. He would not use Saul's enmity for him as an excuse to break covenant with Jonathan or any of his family. David had a perpetual covenant with Jonathan.

WHO'S PURSUING WHOM?

RELIGION IS MAN SEEKING GOD. Christianity isn't about religion, but about relationship. Desiring a covenant relationship with us, God seeks us out. Notice that because of his covenant with Jonathan, David sought out Mephibosheth. David pursued the one with whom he had a covenant of promise.

David's motive was selfless, not selfish. He had nothing to gain by blessing and showing kindness to Mephibosheth except to keep his word—his covenant. So it is with God. He loves us unselfishly and unconditionally. Being in covenant relationship with Him doesn't do anything for God. He does not need us, nor can we do anything for Him. Rather, God pursues us out of *agape*—unconditional love. In fact, He is *driven* to give to us.

I love my wife, Joni, with unconditional love. That means I love her whether or not she acts loving toward me. It also means that I love her whether or not I feel like it. I am in covenant relationship with her through marriage. I have promised to love her "for better or worse." And I am a *driven* husband. I am driven to give: to give her love, material necessities, and every luxury I can lavish upon her. The covenant I have with Joni imparts my every blessing to her.

In a much greater way, God is driven to give to us. His very nature of love compels Him to be a giver.

> God is love. In this was manifested the love of God toward us, that God sent his only begotten Son into the world, that we might live through him. Herein is love, not that we loved God, but that he loved us, and sent his Son to be the propitiation for our sins.
>
> —1 John 4:8b–10

Mephibosheth doesn't look like much to us. He is seemingly small and insignificant in the kingdom of Israel. He has done nothing to merit David's favor or mercy. In fact, all that he received from David was for Jonathan's sake. Doesn't that sound like God's covenant with us? All that He does for us is done for Christ's sake.

Mephibosheth is far from the ideal candidate to receive wealth, abundance, and favor. So are we, for that matter. But God can do so much with so little (1 Kings 18:43–46; 2 Kings 4:1–7). Standing on the top of Mount Carmel after seven years of famine, Elijah's servant saw no sign of rain. For a long time there was nothing. But one day he looked again and saw a small cloud the size of a man's hand beginning to form on the horizon. That little cloud was a lot with God. The widow who came to Elisha first saw nothing and then only a small jar of oil. But that small portion of oil was all God needed to produce continual provision in the midst of famine. Both the servant and the widow had to look again to see divine potential in small beginnings.

Look again at Mephibosheth and then yourself. Though you may not see much, God sees great potential in your position. Yes, Mephibosheth and you may be regarded as "nobodies." But God specializes in making nobodies into somebodies to accomplish His purposes. God says that before He sought us out in Christ, we were those "who in time past were not a people but are now the people of God; who had not obtained mercy but now have obtained mercy" (1 Pet. 2:10).

The covenant of promise cut between David and Jonathan provided for Mephibosheth before he was ever born. The covenant of promise for us in Christ was cut before we were born through His shed blood on the cross. Before you were a thought in your parents' minds, God had already made preparation for your salvation. In Ephesians 1:4–5, Paul says it this way,

> According as he hath chosen us in him before the foundation of the world, that we should be holy and without blame before him in love: having predestinated us unto the adoption of children by Jesus Christ into himself, according to the good pleasure of his will.

Go back with me for a moment to a place just outside of Jerusalem's walls, on a hill called the Place of the Skull. Hear the ringing of the hammer as nails part sinew and flesh. The Father's covenant of promise with the Son existed before birth. So God was seeking us out before we were born to bestow upon us blessing and abundance that we never earned or deserved. We are like Mephibosheth—about to have radical changes made in our lives—from lack to plenty, scarcity to abundance, and from crumbs to a feast.

THE LURE OF LO-DEBAR

TO RECEIVE HIS INHERITANCE, Mephibosheth had to leave Lo-debar. Why would anyone want to stay in such a God-forsaken wilderness? Certainly anywhere would be better for Mephibosheth than Lo-debar.

But a certain lure and attraction emanates from desolation and dryness. Lest you be tempted to stay in your own personal Lo-debar—your own parched pastures where you spend your days groveling for crumbs and leftovers—you must decide now to reject the things that will lure you into Lo-debar:

Living in fear.

Fear pushes us into the darkness of hiding and offers us an escape from reality. The reality is that Mephibosheth is royalty. Yet the memory of his position of royalty has faded in the passing years. Faded are the memories of Jonathan's valor, his grandfather's victories over Israel's enemies, and the covenant of promise between his father and David.

In the forefront of his mind are the painful jeers and mocking gestures made by peers who ridiculed his handicap. As the other boys played, they often invented cruel games to kick his crutches from beneath him and humiliate him on the ground. Then his insensitive playmates would hide his crutches and run off. Unable to pick himself up without assistance, Mephibosheth would lay hopelessly on the ground and sob tears of bitterness until someone finally came to help him home. He is ex-royalty. He fears the outdoors, so he huddles in a dimly lit hut, wasting away life with worry.

Why would such a holy God be interested in you? You have failed to please Him and you feel so undeserving of His love.

Believing the lie.

Fear makes us hide in shadows. Lurking in the shadows are all the lies and half-truths that chain our lives to the past and shatter all our dreams of new tomorrows. Mephibosheth believed the lie that a physical handicap and a sinful ancestor had ruined his potential and promise. So he hid behind the lie and avoided the struggle and pain of facing the truth and changing his life.

What lie are you hiding behind? An abusive relationship? A handicap? A sinful past? An unconfessed, dark sin? An emotional hurt? A mental lapse? Maybe you crawl into the secret world of the Internet and exchange your identity for another. Wrapped in this deceptive game, do you continue to tell yourself the lie that you are nobody and that nobody cares? By believing this lie, you are accepting the curse, and denying your blessing.

Accepting the label of Generation X.

Social commentators have labeled this present generation of youth as Generation X. They are not Baby Boomers or Busters. They have no purpose or direction. No name seems appropriate for this generation of mixed cultures and ideas, so they are simply designated as "X." Mephibosheth may have been the first member of Generation X. Children poked fun at him. Women laughed at him. Men ignored him. He was living in a Jewish ghetto on the outskirts of nowhere—a place called Lo-debar. For him, annihilation or holocaust would have been welcomed. For his was a living hell not inflicted by others but by the prison of his own torturous thoughts. He was "X," ex-royalty.

How horrible that sounds. "Ex" means nobody. As an "ex," you are defined by what you are not instead of by what you are. Allowing the label of "X" you become an ex-spouse, ex-wife, ex-husband, ex-football player, ex-employee, or ex-person. You were somebody, but now you wear the scarlet letter of "X," sown on the fabric of your soul for all to see and scorn.

Lack of knowledge.

Lo-debar is the place where fearful, deceived "X"s live to escape from the real world. They cover themselves in what they are not, never believing that who they are matters to anyone or to God. They go from one addiction after another instead of embracing freedom. They accept pain and hurt, refusing the healing of reconciliation and restoration. They exist in brokenness and sickness, while running from deliverance and health. At times, they use money and material gain, to try to substitute the frigidity of things for the intimacy of relationships. Others seek fulfillment in their work—working all the time to avoid spending time with family or friends. And some hide behind their hate, religion, or prejudices.

Why? Because Hosea 4:6 says, "My people are destroyed for a lack of knowledge."

You may be living in Lo-debar. It is the personal hell of your own creation. Filled with guilt, shame, and worthlessness, you try to hide even from God. Maybe you have been hiding from God, afraid of His holiness and purity. You feel compromised and dirty. His righteousness and truth only serves to expose your filthy rags. For John 8 says, "You shall know the truth and the truth shall set you free."

Fleeing intimidation.

Yes, people may intimidate us. The opinions of others may be more important to us than God's opinion of us. Some love the praise of men more than the praise of God (John 12:43). As a result, they retreat from any criticism or persecution.

They go out of their way to please those they esteem and to placate those they fear. They accept the crutches of humilia-

tion instead of standing firm on the solid support of God's truth. If you find yourself running from intimidation, you will always be crippled by others' opinions of you. The put-downs of others will also put you face down before them, if you flee from their intimidation instead of stand up to it.

> If you find yourself running from intimidation, you will always be crippled by others' opinions of you.

Selling out to your circumstances.

Mephibosheth dwelt in the house of Machir, which means "sold out." He had sold out to his circumstances. Have you ever said, "Well, under the circumstances, I'm doing okay." Who says you are under your circumstances? You are more than a conqueror. You are the head and not the tail. You are above and not beneath. But if your circumstances dictate your lifestyle instead of your position, then you will sell out your birthright for your current situation instead of waiting for your future promise. Living in Machir means that you sell out your palace and live in a hut. You may have settled for less, but God won't.

Like the man with the withered hand, God will demand that you stretch forth your disability (Mark 3:1–5). Perhaps, instead, you are like the prodigal son eating with pigs, but the Father is waiting for you to come to His feast (Luke 15). You may be eating crumbs, but God has prepared His table for you (Luke 16).

YES, YOU CAN RUN from covenant but you cannot hide. The light of His Light will expose you. The Truth of all truth will find you out. You will say with the psalmist,

> If I say, Surely the darkness shall cover me; even the night shall be light about me. Yea, the darkness hideth not from thee, but the night shineth as the day; the darkness and the light are both alike to thee . . . My substance was not hidden from thee. . . .
>
> —Psalm 139:11–12, 15a

Mephibosheth had spent a lifetime hiding out in darkness, existing in fear, deception, nothingness, intimidation, and poverty. But royalty came to him. The covenant of promise outlasted his hopelessness. Lo-debar would not last. Living off of crumbs was but for a season, not for an eternity. His destiny of royalty overtook his handicap of obscurity. It did not matter that Mephibosheth had sunk to the lowest depth known to humanity. One had descended from greatness before his demise to lift him up from the pit and set him on a pinnacle. David—once an outlaw but now the king—searched out Mephibosheth and found him. And now rescued from a meager existence to the banquet hall of royalty,

Living off of crumbs was but for a season, not for an eternity.

Mephibosheth bowed prostrate on the floor before the king, only to discover that the one he had feared the most had loved him more than Mephibosheth could have ever imagined.

THE ROYAL PORTION
BESTOWED ON MEPHIBOSHETH

Peace.

Jerusalem is known all over the world as the City of Peace. Lo-debar is known as the Place of No Pasture. David summoned Mephibosheth to Jerusalem, and the first words he spoke into his ears were "Fear not." These two words are familiar to the writers of Scripture. The prophet Isaiah says, "Fear thou not; for I am with thee: be not dismayed; for I am thy God: I will strengthen thee; yea, I will help thee; yea, I will uphold thee with the right hand of my righteousness" (41:10). When the angel Gabriel appeared to Mary announcing the birth of the coming Messiah his first words were "Fear not." (Luke 1:30). As children of God, we are not to fear but walk in His peace because Luke declares, "Fear not, little flock; for it is your Father's good pleasure to give you the kingdom" (12:32). What is the kingdom? In Romans 14:17, the apostle Paul says, "For the kingdom of God is not meat and drink; but righteousness, and peace, and joy in the Holy Ghost."

When we approach the king's table as the children of God, there is nothing to fear. In fact, we have no anxiety about anything because His peace that passes all understanding guards both our minds and hearts in Christ (Phil. 4:6). Because of the covenant between David and Jonathan, Mephibosheth had nothing to fear. Because of the covenant with the Father sealed by the blood of Christ, we have nothing to fear when we approach God.

Mephibosheth had nothing to fear from the king. We have nothing to fear from our King, God Almighty. We can come into His presence without any feeling of intimidation or dread. One has already gone before us to prepare the way—Christ Jesus. His promise is our boldness, assurance, and confidence: "For God hath not given us the spirit of fear, but of power, and of love, and of a sound mind" (2 Tim. 1:7).

Like clay in the hands of the potter, we may not understand the principle of God's sovereignty or the purpose of His work upon the wheels, but we trust in His person because we know that he would never harm us. Romans 5:1 proclaims that, "Therefore being justified by faith, we have peace with God through our Lord Jesus Christ."

Position.

The second portion Mephibosheth received from the covenant was a position of prominence and honor at the king's table.

> Then said Ziba unto the king, According to all that the lord the king hath commanded his servant, so shall thy servant

do. As for Mephibosheth, he shall eat at my table, as one of the king's sons.

—2 Samuel 8:11

Notice that Mephibosheth is not treated as an alien, stranger, or enemy. Rather, David brought him into his palace and sat him down at his own table to dine.

I believe *The Message* translation of the Bible says it best, "I'll call nobodies and make them somebodies; I'll call the unloved and make them beloved. In the place where they yelled out, 'You're nobody!' they are calling you God's living children" (Rom. 9:25–26).

It is time for you to declare with your own mouth: ***No More Crumbs!*** No longer will you sit under the table begging for any crumbs that might fall your way. Pull out your chair. Spread your napkin. Get out the golden fork and knife. It is time to eat at the King's table. No more malnutrition. No more starvation. No more dry season. You now dine with the King of Kings.

Your position at the King's table is also a good place for you to hide your crippled legs. When Mephibosheth sat at David's table, no one could see his handicap. His position covered his weakness and frailty. Your position in Christ covers your sin, failure, weakness, and frailty. You are in the right position as the King's son to be covered

> Your position in Christ covers your sin, failure, weakness, and frailty.

by His saving, healing, and restoring love. "Behold, what manner of love the Father hath bestowed upon us, that we should be called the sons of God" (1 John 3:1). There is no better position to have in life than to be His child.

> There is no better position in life than to be His child.

You have been adopted into the family of God with all the rights and privileges of a son. John 1:12–13 says,

But as many as received him, to them gave he power to become the sons of God, even to them that believe on his name: Which were born, not of blood, nor of the will of the flesh, nor of the will of man, but of God.

What are these rights?

- According to Ephesians 2:3, you have been translated from one family to another and are no longer a child of wrath.

- According to Ephesians 2:12 and 19 you have been grafted into the family of God.

- According to 1 Peter 2:9, you have been called out of darkness into His marvelous light.

- You are free from all previous family obligations—you are no longer the servant of sin, poverty, and sickness.

- You have all the rights and privileges of the new family—the blood of Jesus, the name of Jesus, the Word of God, and the Holy Spirit.

Provision.

Not only did Mephibosheth have peace and position, he also was given provision under the covenant. He was shown kindness by David for Jonathan's sake. What Mephibosheth had amounted to was so very little—rags, crutches, and lameness. But in the covenant, he had every provision he needed. God is able to do much with so little.

Remember the boy's lunch that Jesus used to feed five thousand hungry people? The few loaves and fishes were so little, but God did so much with it. Elijah's servant only saw a cloud the size of a man's hand, but out of such a small thing God produced a great rain. In a borrowed stable and manger, a baby wrapped in swaddling clothes looked like so little, but God did much with that baby who was the King of Kings and Lord of Lords.

Do you remember the Generation X label that I pointed out earlier? Do not let your future be determined by your past. Your future is determined by your provision under the New Covenant of Christ. The steadfast love of the Lord never ceases. Under his covenant of love everything that Jesus won on the cross belongs now to every child of the King.

Notice what happened to Mephibosheth. He had nothing in his own wealth, but he had an abundant provision under the covenant. David restored all of Saul's land to him because of the covenant. Imagine the weathered and beaten face of Mephibosheth. In that face, David was reminded of Mephibosheth's grandfather, Saul, the anointed king of Israel. In that face David was also reminded of his covenant brother, Jonathan, whom he loved with his whole heart.

Your future is determined by your provision under the New Covenant of Christ.

We are born of the incorruptible seed of the Word of God. When the Father looks at you and me, He sees just enough of the features of His slain Son on Calvary that He is reminded of the everlasting covenant we have in Christ. And God desires to bestow His kindness upon you for the sake of Christ.

The provision of David's covenant restored every provision to Mephibosheth. Restoration is an integral part of provision. And repentance brings restoration. "Repent, therefore, and be converted, that your sins may be blotted out, when the times of refreshing shall come from the presence of the Lord" (Acts 3:19). If you will repent by changing your mind and direction from the world back to God, then the refreshing of God's restoration will come into your life. God will restore to you the years that the locusts have eaten. He will restore your health, wealth, joy, victory, peace, and all the provisions that you need.

Repent and confess exactly who you are. Jacob confessed that he was a deceiver and supplanter, and God restored him. Mephibosheth had to appear in David's palace as the person he was. There was no pretense or position when he arrived. All he had were his rags and his lameness. Before we can receive the provision of God's covenant in Christ for our lives, we must first repent. We must cry out, "Change me, God. I am an unworthy sinner. But I repent of my sin and receive Christ as my Savior. He alone is my provision."

Listen to this promise: "Thou preparest a table before me in the presence of mine enemies; thou anointest my head with oil; my cup runneth over" (Ps. 23:5).

Perpetual Privilege.

David promised Mephibosheth that he would eat bread at the king's table continually (2 Sam. 8:7). The privilege that Mephibosheth had at David's table was perpetual and everlasting. In the upcoming chapters, we will discover that we are living in a time when the reapers will overtake the sowers. Time is being so shortened that we will sow with one hand and reap with the other. God will send the

> **Before we can receive the provision of God's covenant in Christ for our lives, we must first repent.**

former and latter rains together, and there will be no more dry season. Every day for the rest of his life, Mephibosheth will enjoy the privileges of sitting at David's table. Provision will be continually there for him.

Here is the problem that so many people face. Mephibosheth possessed the covenant privileges when he was in Lo-debar, but he did not act upon them. The elder son in the parable of the Loving Father (Luke 15) had the continual blessings of the Father, but he did not know it. He could have killed the fatted calf at any time but he did not act upon the perpetual privileges that were his. Jesus tells us that as soon as the harvest is ripe—as soon as the privilege is available—we must put our sickle to the harvest (Mark 4:29).

It is time that we learned to harvest. It is time to leave Lo-debar, come out of the howling wilderness, the parched pastures, and the slums of crumbs, and take our position at the King's table. No matter what others say about us or how they laugh, mock, or taunt us, we must begin to walk in our perpetual privilege as God's children.

> It is time to leave Lo-debar, come out of the howling wilderness, the parched pastures, and the slums of crumbs, and take our position at the King's table.

Promised Harvest

A friend of mine from South Dakota, who is a farmer, shared with me recently a story about one of his crops. He told me his last harvest was terrible. More than one third of his crops rotted in the field because his harvest time was cut short by early snows that buried his fields and ruined his harvest. How many answers to your prayers have been in the fields, but you were not quick enough to harvest? You may have waited at home for someone to bring your answer to you. All the while, the answer to your prayer was standing tall in the fields ready to provide you with God's provision, but you were too late, too lazy, or too disobedient to put the sickle in to reap your harvest.

The harvest is continually there not only for us, but for our households and children. You and I must refuse to tarry. We must leave an inheritance—a spiritual heritage and a financial blessing—to our children. Will you claim your perpetual privilege and bring in the harvest, or will you miss the harvest and have your prayer crop rot in the field?

Mephibosheth received a royal portion from King David as the result of a covenant between David and Jonathan. That covenant foreshadowed the covenant that King Jesus made with us. We no longer have to live in

> How many answers to your prayers have been in the fields, but you were not quick enough to harvest?

Lo-debar. Through the blood of Christ, we are now partakers in a new covenant under which we can declare, *No More Crumbs!* Here is the royal portion bestowed upon us by the King of Kings:

- *Peace.* No longer does fear keep us in bondage. Through Christ we have peace with God, and we can enter into the blessings of the new covenant.

- *Position.* Our position in Christ is that we are the

children of God. As His children, we are royalty and at His table our sin and lameness is covered by His grace.

- *Provision.* Through repentance and confession of sin, we enter into the abundant provision of Christ, assured that He will supply every need through His riches in glory.

- *Perpetual Privilege.* As children of God, we can enjoy the privilege of eating at the King's table every day for the rest of our lives.

- *Promised Harvest.* The harvest is ready and waiting for us. We must not sit back but should quickly put the sickle to the harvest and claim all that God has for us. It is time to lay hold of the harvest and not to leave the crop in the field.

Now we will turn to the life of Elijah and discover how he implemented the principle of sowing in famine in order to overcome famine. If you feel that you are at the end of your resources and have nothing left to give and no hope to receive your much needed answer, then keep reading. Your harvest is just around the corner.

3

Preparing for Your Harvest

THE HAIRY MAN burst into the royal court before
anyone could stop him. He was dressed in roughly
tailored animal skins, girded with a leather belt. His
eyes blazed with an unearthly fire. The guards who normally
stopped all intruders seemed paralyzed with fear—not the
fear of man but rather the fear of God.

Ahab, king of Israel, had never encountered such a man.
Of course, his court was filled with his own prophets who
always spoke pleasing, comforting words that soothed his
seared conscience and placated any twinge of guilt.

"Who is this rude intruder?" King Ahab demanded of
the royal counselor standing by his side.

"Elijah, the Tishbite from Gilead," the counselor curtly responded, his words dripping with scorn and contempt.

"Why is he here uninvited in my court?" Ahab angrily snapped.

But before the king's counselor could reply, Elijah stopped right in front of the king. Dead silence filled the room. The smell of sweat mingled with dirt and animal odor emanated from him. No perfume covered his earthy fragrance. No razor had touched his flowing hair and beard. And his eyes burned with a fire that Ahab had never seen. His very presence radiated a glow and power that had been absent in Israel for decades.

Everyone in Ahab's royal court suddenly felt naked, as if every sinful thought and action were clearly exposed. There was a holiness about Elijah that unmasked every pretense and revealed every sin. Beads of sweat flowed from the brows of each man standing in the court, including Ahab. Although everyone desired to get out of the room as soon as possible, a spiritual weight they had never before encountered glued each person to his spot on the polished, sandstone floor. Face-to-face—the prophet's blazing eyes piercing the guilty ones of Ahab—Elijah opened his mouth to speak.

IN THE SPLIT SECOND before Elijah spoke, which seemed like an eternity, King Ahab's mind raced through the events of his sordid past. Though a descendant of King David, he was far from a man with a heart for God. In fact, Ahab had done more evil in God's sight than all those who had gone before him in the rebellious Northern Kingdom of Israel. After Solomon's death, the kingdom had split in two, with Judah continuing to worship God in the Temple at Jerusalem and Israel making her own idolatrous sites of worship at Bethel and Dan. In fact, every pagan high place in Israel was dedicated to images and idols for worship. The idolatrous Israelites worshiped everything from golden calves to dead ancestors instead of the living God.

Ahab had married Jezebel, the daughter of Ethbaal—king of the wicked Sidonians. Under her influence, Ahab built a temple to Baal in Samaria and worshipped this idol openly with his wicked wife.

Deep within, Ahab knew that God was filled with righteous wrath against him and his kingdom. But what could God do? Israel was much mightier now and much more prosperous than weak Judah. God was powerless to challenge the mighty Ahab, or so he thought. But for some reason, this wild-looking prophet who now stood before him caused a chill to penetrate his bones. He began to tremble inside with a fear stronger than any he had ever felt.

A dread of Yahweh, the God of Abraham, Isaac, and Jacob, started deep within his soul and infected every muscle fiber, causing him to tremble and shake as never before. No encounter with Baal had done anything like this to him. He left his worship of Baal feeling cold and distant. But this was a very different feeling. A fire waxed in his bones. His hard heart seemed to melt like butter. This prophet, Elijah, who stood before him had a presence about him like no other man Ahab had ever met. With a sense of awe and dread, Ahab leaned forward in his throne, sensing that what he was about to hear was not just from a man, but from God Himself.

WITH A BOOMING VOICE that sounded like thunder, Elijah spoke directly to the king. No polite introductions. No words of flattery. Elijah's words struck like a hammer smashing down on hot metal to be shaped on an anvil. "As the Lord God of Israel lives, before whom I stand, there shall not be dew nor rain these years, but according to my word."

Ahab opened his mouth to respond, but it was too late. As soon as the pronouncement had left Elijah's mouth, the prophet turned and ran from the court, disappearing just as suddenly as he had appeared. No one knew what to make of it. Some began to laugh nervously. Others started to mock and deride the unkempt prophet, mimicking his words and actions. But Ahab said nothing. Something deep inside of him told him that this wasn't the last time he would face Elijah. Ahab knew that truth rang in this prophet's words. There was nothing he could do to change anything about his life. He felt trapped by his domineering, idolatrous wife and a national destiny bent on rejecting God and worshipping Baal. The only course of action left open to him was to sit and wait. If this wild-eyed prophet truly spoke for God, time would verify whether or not Elijah had spoken the truth.

AS ELIJAH FLED from the court, he felt dirty all over. He had never before experienced the sinful, ominous wickedness that he felt in that place. Like the smell of smoke that lingers in every garment it touches, Elijah could literally smell the stench of iniquity oozing like pus from an infected boil. The nation once known as the chosen people of Almighty God was now an overflowing cesspool of wicked thoughts and actions. He longed to run to a rushing river and scrub himself clean, confessing to God every sin he had discerned in the court.

He knew that he was a nobody who was now an enemy of the most powerful man in Israel, Yet, strangely, he felt no fear.

While running at top speed, Elijah heard God's voice explode into his consciousness. "Get from here. Turn east. Hide by the brook Cherith, which is before the Jordan. There you will drink of the brook. There I have commanded ravens to feed you."

As Elijah ran toward the brook Cherith, he pondered the provision of God. He knew that he was a nobody who was now an enemy of the most powerful man in Israel. Yet, strangely, he felt no fear. A peace filled his soul like never before. As odd as it may seem, he also felt himself to be in a position of power greater than any earthly king. And though he was a nobody in his own eyes and the eyes of others, God had chosen in grace to provide for his every need. It seemed as though an endless, continual blessing poured from heaven into his life. He knew that in the midst of famine in the land, he would sow faithfulness and obedience into his relationship with Yahweh. He knew that somehow a harvest awaited him unlike any man had ever experienced.

An image of Enoch of old filled his mind. Enoch had simply walked from this life to the next without tasting death. Whenever Elijah thought of Enoch, an unspeakable joy filled his heart. Deep within him flowed a God-inspired hope that, like Enoch, he would never taste death. That promise empowered him to speak whatever God commanded and to do whatever God required. So he ran quickly to the brook where God had commanded him to go. He was ready to be refreshed and to experience God's provision.

FOR A SEASON, Elijah hid at the brook Cherith, but then the drought that covered Israel caused the waters to run dry. Again God spoke to Elijah. "Go to Zarephath in Sidon. I will provide for you there."

Immediately Elijah traveled to the city. As he approached the outskirts of the village, he noticed a widow who was gathering sticks.

"Fetch me a drink of water in your pot that I may drink," Elijah requested.

As she turned to go for water, Elijah continued, "I pray you, also bring me a morsel of bread."

Stopping and turning back to Elijah with a tone of despair in her voice, she answered, "As God liveth, I have no bread, but only a handful of flour in a barrel, and just a small amount of oil. So I am gathering a few sticks for a fire to cook our last bit of food. Once my son and I eat it, we will be ready to die."

The time had come for this desperate widow to learn the lesson of sowing in famine. She would soon experience how God is able to do much with only a little. Elijah spoke an incredible word of promise, "Fear not. Make me some bread first and then make bread for you and your son. I tell you that God has said that you will not run out of flour or oil until the day that God again sends forth rain for the land."

> The time had come for this desperate widow to learn the lesson of sowing in famine.

Marveling at his words, the widow quickly returned to her house. Limp, wasted, and malnourished, her son slumped over in the corner of her house with life slowly ebbing from his frail frame. She started the fire from her twigs and poured all the oil into the pan. Emptying the rest of her meal into the pan, she kneaded the dough into a small loaf and cooked the bread on her earthen stove.

With her first loaf of pan-fried bread completed, she picked up the empty jar of oil and began to pour. To her amazement, just enough oil came out to make one more loaf. Her heart pounding, she emptied the barrel of meal into the pan and just enough flour flowed out to make one loaf of bread. The poor widow began to laugh as she cooked the second loaf. Never before had she experienced such over-whelming joy. Her laughter became a wellspring within her soul as she experienced firsthand the miracle harvest before her eyes.

Upon baking the second loaf and giving it to her aston-ished son, she ran to the prophet with water and bread. The two exchanged a knowing look. He instantly saw the joy in her eyes and knew God's promised provision had arrived.

After eating and drinking until they were full, Elijah stayed at the widow's house. Each day, the three of them ate the perpetual provision from the Lord. Like the children of Israel wandering in the wilderness who fed upon the manna that God provided each day, these three souls living in Zarephath trusted His provision and reaped a promised harvest in the midst of famine.

IN SPITE OF God's continual blessing, the widow feared the day the provision would stop and she and her son would return to the state of lack and poverty. Like Mephibosheth, they had lived so long in their own Lo-debar that their faith was weak and their hope hung only by a slight thread.

Like a self-fulfilling prophecy, her unspoken fear materi-alized suddenly one day when her beloved son fell sick. He shook violently with fever, and without warning, stopped breathing.

With overwhelming grief, she cried out to Elijah, "What have I to do with you? O man of God! Have you come to me to call my sin to remembrance and to slay my son?"

Without hesitation, Elijah had the widow bring him the boy, and he laid the dead child on his own bed. Crying out to God, Elijah prayed with a loud voice, "O Lord my God, why have You brought evil on this widow with whom I am living to kill her son?"

Elijah continued to pray fervently as he laid on top of the boy. After crying out to God three times, Elijah felt a shudder beneath him. The boy began to cough and struggled to get out from under the weight of Elijah. Life again flowed through the boy's frail body.

Elijah carried the restored child into the widow's main room and declared, "See, your son lives."

With overwhelming joy and relief, the widow exclaimed, "Now I know you are a man of God and His truth is in your mouth."

Again hope stirred within Elijah. As he walked away, he thought of Enoch again. For a moment he pondered leaving this world with all its troubles and difficulties and crossing over to a new life with God. No sooner had he meditated on such glory than another thought crossed his mind. This second thought was frightful and foreboding. Soon he would have to face the evil Ahab. What would God require? Would the dry season ever end and rain once again fall on the developing desert of Israel?

He left the widow's hut and began to run. Running was his release when he felt burdened by heavy thoughts. As Elijah ran, the arid wind flowed though his hair and beard. He felt free and unfettered by worries and cares. He continued to run off into the sunset, hoping to meet God and never having to return. But the time for such a meeting had not yet arrived. He would soon face the greatest challenge of his life. Again a sense of great foreboding welled up within him, and the prophet ran with greater intensity into the starry night, praying all the while as he ran.

AT LAST THE DAY CAME when God spoke again to Elijah. "Go, face Ahab, and I will send rain upon the earth."

Meeting Obadiah on his way back to Samaria, Elijah said to the faithful prophet of God who oversaw Ahab's household, "Go tell Ahab that Elijah has returned. And after you tell him, the Spirit of God will carry you to a place you know not so that Ahab cannot find you."

With great fear, Obadiah obediently went to tell Ahab. The evil King Ahab set out immediately to find Elijah. When they finally met again, Ahab was the first to speak. "So here you are. You are the one that troubles Israel."

Elijah responded, "No, King, you are the one. You and your father's house have broken the commands of the Lord. You now worship Baal instead of the living God. So go now and gather your four hundred and fifty prophets of Baal on Mount Carmel. Let all those false prophets who eat at

Jezebel's table come. We will see there on the mountain if Baal is truly God or if the Lord God is truly God."

Ready to humiliate Elijah and rid himself of this thorn in the flesh, King Ahab summoned all the prophets of Baal and the people to gather on Mount Carmel. This would be the final showdown with Elijah. Ahab was confident that Elijah would be disgraced, and then he could stone the prophet and get him out of the way once and for all.

Thousands of people gathered on the mountain to watch this bizarre showdown between a solitary prophet of Yahweh named Elijah and the formidable host of prophets who worshipped Baal. Like her evil husband, Queen Jezebel also relished this moment when her accuser would be defeated by the magic spells and sorcery of her cultic prophets.

The crowd gathered on the mountain, anxiously awaiting the arrival of Elijah. Without warning, the burly prophet pushed his way through the crowd and thundered, "How long will you have divided loyalties? Either Yahweh is God or Baal is. You must decide." The crowd became deathly silent.

"Give us two bulls. One is for Baal's prophets and the other for me. Baal's prophets will go first. Let them cut up one of the bulls and lay the pieces on their altar. Put no fire under it. Call upon the name of your god, and we will see if Baal answers by fire. And I will call upon the name of the Lord. Whichever God answers by fire then that one is God," Elijah demanded.

The crowd immediately thundered, "It is well!"

For several hours, the prophets of Baal danced around their altar, pleading with their god to send fire. Occasionally Elijah would taunt them, "Perhaps Baal is asleep or gone on vacation. Shout louder! Dance harder!" And so their hysteria built with screams and shouts and ever louder cries. But nothing happened. In desperation, they even cut themselves in an attempt to invoke Baal's pity. Still nothing happened. Exhausted, they finally collapsed on the ground, completely spent in the kind of human delirium that inspires passionate religion but never reaches the heart of the one and only true God.

An eerie calm filled the air, like the stillness that precedes a violent storm. Dark clouds began to gather over the mountain's crest. With a serenity that stood in stark contrast to the false prophets' behavior, Elijah beckoned the crowd, "Come near to me." The people, with fearful expectation, inched forward toward the strange prophet. Taking twelve stones, one for each tribe of Israel, Elijah built an altar to Yahweh. He dug a deep trench around the altar, cut up a bull into pieces, and laid the strips of meat across the wood on top of the altar.

> Those with hearts hardened toward the Spirit of God can never discern His approach or hear His voice.

Then the prophet of God commanded those standing close to him to pour four barrels of water on the altar. He ordered the same drenching a second and third time, until the trench around the altar's base was filled with water.

As the sun slowly descended in the west and preparations were being made for the time of the evening sacrifice, the rough-hewn prophet spoke in a quiet voice, quite uncharacteristic of the bombastic oracles he earlier delivered to Ahab. In a barely audible voice, Elijah reverently spoke his prayer. "Lord God of Abraham, Isaac, and Jacob, let it be known this day that You alone are God in Israel and that all I have done has been according to Your word. Hear me, O God."

Suddenly fire fell from heaven and consumed the sacrifice, the wood, the altar, and boiled the water in the trench so that immediately it vaporized into a cloud of steam. Without hesitation, the whole crowd fell on their faces, crying out with fear and awe, "The Lord God Jehovah, He alone is God!"

Then Elijah thundered his command, "Take every prophet of Baal and kill them now. They are false prophets and deserving of death by the law of Almighty God."

That evening, four hundred and fifty soothsayers lay slain on top of Mount Carmel.

FROM HIS THRONE under the royal canopy, Ahab had watched the day's proceedings with increasing horror. When he saw all of Baal's prophets slaughtered, he began to dread Jezebel's anger more than the power of God. *How will I tell her?* he desperately wondered.

As he pondered all his upcoming problems with the queen, Elijah stormed into Ahab's tent, interrupting the king's private musings.

"Get up. Eat and drink. For there is the sound of the abundance of rain coming," warned Elijah.

Ahab did not respond. Those with hearts hardened toward the Spirit of God can never discern His approach or hear His voice. King Ahab was so hungry that he began to devour his evening meal while Elijah climbed up the mountain with his servant. Reaching a quiet spot, Elijah knelt on the rocky soil and put his face between his knees. Prostrate before God, he prayed for Him to open the heavens as He had promised.

ELIJAH'S TIME OF SOWING in the midst of famine had been completed. He had sown everything—his faith, his obedience, even to the point of risking his life for the Lord. Like the widow with just a bit of oil and meal, he had nothing left to give God but his life. And that wasn't much. He was nothing in his own eyes, and he knew that the Israelites' promised loyalty to God would soon vanish under Jezebel's wrath, as the dew is consumed by the scorching morning sun.

The peace that filled his heart, though, overcame his fear that God might not send rain. In that moment of sincere prayer, his position before the Lord was secure. He was a man of God, and no earthly or spiritual enemy could ever defeat him. Elijah had experienced divine provision at the brook where he was fed by ravens and at the home of the widow who had a perpetual supply of food in the midst of famine. He had the privilege of seeing the mighty God of

Israel answer his prayer before thousands of witnesses by raining down fire upon his altar. Only one portion of the royal blessing remained to be fulfilled—the promised harvest.

God had promised to send abundant rain to irrigate the fields and bring forth an end to the dry season blanketing the land. As Elijah prayed, he desperately longed for the promise of God to be fulfilled. He had done all he had been commanded to do. Now the situation was out of his hands.

God's miraculous power starts where our human strength ends. When we have done all that God requires, we must then patiently wait for His provision. Now it was Elijah's time to wait and believe that God would do much with a little—a little faith, a little obedience, and a little prayer. Elijah had sown everything he had, believing God would

> When we have done all that God requires, we must then patiently wait for His provision.

end the famine and bring the promised harvest. Would his faithful God act now? Only by waiting would Elijah see the promised harvest. But how long would he have to wait?

4

Look Again

ON MOUNT CARMEL, Elijah fell prostrate with his face between his knees as he cried out to God to send the downpour of rain. After what seemed to be hours, Elijah sent his servant to go look toward the sea and report his findings. Six times the servant went and looked toward the sea. Six times he saw nothing. There was no excitement in his voice and nothing to produce hope of rain. The sky was as cloudless as it had been for the past seven years.

Without perseverance, we can never hope to experience the perpetual privilege of being God's children or receiving His harvest. God promised Elijah that He would send rain.

So Elijah was holding on to God until His promise was fulfilled. He would not let go. Just like the woman with the issue of blood persisted in her pursuit of Jesus, crawling on the ground under the legs of many in a crowd just to touch the hem of His garment, so Elijah got down on his knees and persistently sought God until He acted. As Smith Wigglesworth often said, "I will not move until God moves." We, as believers, need such pitbull faith and tenacity.

> When we have done all that we can in obedience, we must persist in faith and prayer, standing firm against all attacks of fear and doubt until God fulfills His promise.

When we have done all that we can in obedience, we must persist in faith and prayer, standing firm against all attacks of fear and doubt until God fulfills His promise.

So Elijah stood firm. In persistent prayer he bombarded heaven until his answer manifested. His circumstances attempted to cloud his reason and the only "sign" of rain was the seemingly insignificant prophecy Elijah pronounced to King Ahab only hours earlier. But the man of God chose to walk by faith and not by sight (2 Cor. 5:7).

One more time, Elijah sent his servant to spy out the sky. Standing on the precipice of Mount Carmel for the seventh time, the number of completion, the weather-beaten assistant saw a tiny cloud no bigger than a man's hand. That was it! The evidence of God's promised harvest had appeared. For people of faith and prayer, it doesn't take much for them to prepare for the harvest. After all, God does much with a little. All He needs is a mustard seed of faith. All God needs is a little oil and flour. All God needs is persistent prayer. All God needs is a little cloud. God can always do so much with so little.

Nothing had changed with Elijah's immediate surroundings and circumstances. The arid, dry winds still swept across Mount Carmel. Dust still filled his nostrils, beard, hair, and clothes. The parched pastures of Lo-debar still engulfed the nation of Israel. But there was a small cloud far in the west rising over the Mediterranean. No man except a man of faith and prayer who was not afraid to look again could have seen a downpour of rain in that tiny cloud.

The promised harvest came *suddenly*. God is doing a quick work in these last days from the time of sowing to reaping. In Jesus' ministry, people were healed and delivered *suddenly*. At Pentecost, *suddenly* the room in which the disciples were praying in one accord was filled with Holy Ghost wind and fire.

In the same moment that Elijah saw the tiny cloud, he sent a warning to Ahab. "Prepare your chariot. Get down off the mountain. Go home now so that the rain will not stop you." Ahab had no faith or prayer. He too could have seen the tiny cloud and thought nothing of it. Without faith and prayer, no man can see the promised harvest of God. So Ahab could only rely on the prophet's warning: *Get going . . . rain is coming!*

Suddenly, in the time that Elijah's servant ran to tell King Ahab, the heavens turned black with clouds that poured out a great flood. Ahab pounded his horses, driving his chariot hard and fast toward Jezreel. And Elijah was so empowered by the hand of the Lord fulfilling His promise that he was able to run ahead of Ahab's chariot into the city.

> # Without faith and prayer, no man can see the promised harvest of God.

THE COMING HARVEST

WE MUST PREPARE. God's coming harvest of salvation and abundance will appear suddenly. Are you ready?

> And he [Jesus] said, "So is the kingdom of God, as if a man should cast seed into the ground. And should sleep, and rise night and day, and the seed should spring and grow up, he knoweth not how. For the earth bringeth forth fruit of herself: first the blade, then the ear, after that the full corn in the ear. But when the fruit is brought forth, immediately he putteth in the sickle, because the harvest is come."
>
> —Mark 4:26–29

The earth does what it was created to do—nurture the seed. The created purpose and nature of the seed is to reproduce after it has been germinated by the soil. Soil always tries to germinate seed. Put a post in the ground, and after a period of time it will rot because the soil is trying to germinate it. "While the earth remaineth, seed time and harvest, and cold and heat, and summer and winter, and day and night shall not cease" (Gen. 8:22). Life is in the seed and nourishment is in the soil. And when the fruit comes forth, suddenly the sower moves in with a sickle to harvest.

How long does the sower wait for the harvest? Not long! Listen to this amazing truth revealed in Amos 9:13:

> Behold, the days come," saith the Lord, "that the plowman shall overtake the reaper, and the treader of grapes him that soweth seed; and the mountains shall drop sweet wine, and all the hills shall melt.

Do you see it? The sower will overtake the reaper. God's promised harvest is that sowing and reaping will happen at the same time. Souls and abundance to the saints is coming quicker than we can preach, or sow. Time is caught up in an accelerated process. "Then shalt thou call, and the Lord shall answer; thou shalt cry, and he shall say, Here I am" (Isa. 58:9a). Notice the immediacy of God's response. God will respond suddenly when we cry out as Elijah did.

The closer we get to the end of the age and the imminent return of Jesus, the shorter time becomes. The time is coming when there will only be seed time and harvest. In fact, the time is coming when seed time and harvest will be the same time.

Not only will we reap what we sow suddenly, but God will also give seed to the sowers and multiply their seed. "Now he that ministereth seed to the sower both minister bread for your food, and multiply your seed sown, and increase the fruit of your righteousness" (2 Cor. 9:10). That means that whenever we sow seed, God comes behind us and sows more. So when we go to harvest, we are not just harvesting what we have sown but also what God has sown as well. He brings such multiplication and increase to our sowing that before our seed can hit the ground, we are reaping a harvest.

A friend of mine once took me fishing once off the coast of Florida. We had been out on his boat for hours with not so much as a nibble. I thought sarcastically to myself, *Well, we are sure having fun now!*

All of a sudden, my friend pushed the throttle down, and we went soaring across the water. I asked him, "Where are we going in such a hurry?" He replied, "Over to that log." What I didn't know is that fish like to congregate around logs, wood, and other things floating in the water. He urged, "Hurry, cast your line in."

No sooner did our lines hit the water than the fish were biting on our bait. This went on for nearly thirty minutes. By this time we were running out of bait. I said, "Why don't we try cutting up one of these fish and see if they will still bite? I think they're so hungry they'll bite on an idea right now!" We cut up a fish and began to cast it out into the water, but before our bait even touched the water, a huge fish jumped up and grabbed it!

That is what is going to happen in these last days. Before your seed can leave one hand you are going to be reaping with the other!

What are we to be sowing? We must sow joy into the life of someone filled with sorrow. We are to sow hope into the middle of a hopeless situation. We should bless someone who needs a blessing without any expectation of their gratitude or giving back to us. We need to sow money into the good soil of God's work, knowing that He will bring a great harvest of souls. We should not only sow in good times but also in times of famine, so that we may reap a bountiful harvest in spite of the dry season we may be experiencing.

The widow sowed in famine and saw God provide a perpetual harvest. Elijah sowed in the midst of a dry season and saw God bring forth a great rain. Are you sowing in your famine as well as your abundance?

It is God's will that His saints prosper. John 10:10 proclaims, "The thief cometh not, but for to steal, and to kill, and to destroy: I am come that they might have life, and that they might have it more abundantly."

WHAT KEEPS US FROM LOOKING AGAIN?

SINCE GOD HAS GIVEN us *peace* to prepare the field; *position* to sow the seed; *provision* to sow in an accelerated time; the *perpetual privilege* of always having from Him more seed to sow; and a *promised harvest* from sowing, then why do we not sow?

Fear.

We might call fear: **F**alse **E**vidence that **A**ppears **R**eal. In others words, fear springs from the lies of the enemy and the world. Fear is a mirage from Satan. He attacks us with difficult circumstances that we feel in the natural we can never get through.

But the Bible says, "For we walk by faith and not by sight" (2 Cor. 5:7). We must not react to our circumstances. Instead, we should respond to every circumstance with faith, being content in what God is doing in and through us. Paul wrote about the attitude that we need: "I know both how to be abased, and I know how to abound; everywhere and in all things I am instructed both to be full and to be hungry, both to abound and to suffer need" (Phil. 4:12).

We are not to be moved in fear by what we see or feel. We fix our eyes on Jesus. We do not look at false evidence that appears to be real. Instead, we stand on the Word of God. So when our body screams that we are sick, we scream back that we are well. When our finances say that we don't have a cent to our name, we declare that we will sow in famine, that there is no dry season, and that we will no longer settle for crumbs. Isaiah 41:10 declares, "Fear thou not; for I am with thee; be not dismayed; for I am thy God: I will strengthen thee; yea,

I will help thee; yea, I will uphold thee with the right hand of my righteousness."

Fear and faith are opposites. They cannot live in the same heart. One will destroy the other. Remember that Abraham was strong in faith because he did not waver between faith and fear. "He [Abraham] staggered not at the promise of God through unbelief, but was strong in faith, giving glory to God, and being fully persuaded that, what he [God] had promised, he was able to perform" (Rom. 4:20–21). Now the word "stagger" actually refers to "vacillate," which literally means "to slide between two mutually exclusive objects." Fear slides us off of faith and into doubt and unbelief.

> ## Fear and faith are opposites. They cannot live in the same heart. One will destroy the other.

Don't worry about tomorrow. Do not become anxious about what you will need. Sow today as God gives you seed and opportunity. Cast out fear. Say, "Spirit of fear, in the name of Jesus, I cast you out. I refuse to be controlled by fear and doubt."

Greed.

If we are afraid to let go of what is in our hand, we will never reap a harvest. Jesus declares in Luke 6:38, "Give and it shall be given unto you." We can never receive until we give. We can never harvest until we sow. There must be the process of exchange. Everything belongs to God. We are simply stewards, or caretakers, of what is His. When He tells us in Malachi 3 that we should tithe and He will rebuke the devourer, that is exactly what we must do with His money. Greed not only says, *What's mine belongs to me.* Greed goes further by saying, *What's yours is mine.*

> We can never receive until we give. We can never harvest until we sow. There must be the process of exchange.

When you take from God, you end up owing Him both what you stole and twenty percent on top of that! "And if a man will at all redeem ought of his tithes, he shall add thereto the fifth part thereof (Lev. 27:31). Your greed will cost you heavily. But as you bind fear and greed, and allow love to motivate your giving, you will receive a bountiful harvest.

STANDING FIRM ON THE TRUTH
IN SPITE OF THE FACTS

WE CAN LEARN from Isaac the principle of standing and sowing in the midst of famine and our present circumstances.

> And there was a famine in the land, besides the first famine that was in the days of Abraham. And Isaac went unto Abimelech king of the Philistines unto Gerar. And the Lord

appeared unto him, and said, "Go not down into Egypt; dwell in the land which I shall tell thee of. Sojourn in the land, and I will be with thee, and will bless thee; for unto thee, and unto thy seed, I will give all these countries, and I will perform the oath which I sware unto Abraham thy father." . . . Then Isaac sowed in that land, and received in the same year an hundredfold: and the Lord blessed him.

—Genesis 26:12

Principle 1: Sow when times are tough.

Our natural tendency is to hold on tight to what we have when lack attacks. But the wise steward knows that there will be no harvest without first sowing. If we refuse to give in our lack, we will never experience the promised harvest. The truth of sowing and reaping remains constant in abundance and in scarcity. Whatever we sow, we will reap. If we sow to famine, we will reap a famine. If we sow to abundance, then we will reap a bountiful harvest.

> **If we refuse to give in our lack, we will never experience the promised harvest.**

Principle 2: Don't eat your seed.

Remember the story about the widow in Zarephath? She knew that if she and her son decided to eat their last oil and meal, then they would die.

75

And she said, As the Lord thy God liveth, I have not a cake, but an handful of meal in a barrel, and a little oil in a cruse: and behold, I am gathering two sticks, that I may go in and dress it for me and my son, that we may eat it, and die.

—1 Kings 17:12

Now if she had eaten the last of her seed, she and her son certainly would have died. But she had another option. She could sow her seed instead of eating it. She could make a loaf of bread for the man of God, Elijah, and then see the promised harvest from God. Her obedience to God's command through Elijah brought her perpetual and promised harvest.

When Elijah asked her for a cake, at first the poor widow claimed that she didn't have it. But God never asks you for what you don't have. He only asks you for what you want to keep for yourself. Remember, if what is in your hand is not big enough to be your harvest, then count on it being your seed. Elijah rebuked the fear in the woman and told her to give what she had. In return, God supplied what she needed—a promised harvest of ever-increasing grain and oil.

> **But God never asks you for what you don't have. He only asks for what you want to keep for yourself.**

Principle 3: Lay hold of God's Word.

What God promises, He always does. The widow was promised a perpetual supply of meal and grain until the famine ended. And God did exactly what He promised.

God promises us that when we give, we receive back "good measure, pressed down, and shaken together, and running over, shall men give into your bosom. For with the same measure that ye mete it shall be measured to you again" (Luke 6:38).

In Genesis 39–51, we read the story of Jacob and Joseph. God promised His provision, privilege, and harvest to Joseph in a dream. But Joseph had to wait many years to receive his inheritance. Through slavery, false accusations, prison, and repeated disappointment, Joseph never gave up. Why? Because he had a Word from God. He laid hold of that promise and would not let go. He persevered. That means he refused to quit. You have God's Word for a promised harvest. So then, don't quit!

Jacob also had God's Word to supply all of his needs through the covenant God had made with his grandfather, Abraham. The day came that Joseph's promise from God was fulfilled. Pharaoh made Joseph second in command over all of Egypt and entrusted him to build storehouses for grain during the seven good years to prepare for the coming seven years of famine.

So Jacob, during the years of terrible famine, sent his sons into Egypt to find food. Joseph disguised himself and met with his brothers. He sent wagons laden with food for his father, Jacob. Jacob had sent empty wagons to Egypt, but because of God's covenant with him, they returned full. Your wagons are coming. Don't quit!

On a word from the Lord, Peter stepped over the side of a boat tossing in a storm on the Sea of Galilee, and he began walking on water toward Jesus. But when he saw the wind and the waves, he became afraid and started to sink. At first, faith had silenced all fear and doubt. But then Peter took His eyes off of the Word and started listening to his own fearful voices that spoke False Evidence that Appeared Real. So Peter sank. He had forgotten God's Word. Now, is it any harder to walk on water in a storm than in the sunshine? Of course not! What made it hard to walk on water was Peter's fear.

How do you sow in famine? By remembering God's Word, no matter what your situation or circumstance. By refusing to take your eyes off his promise and not being afraid to look again. Let this be the straight path of moving to no more crumbs:

- Do not doubt the Word of God.

- Do not listen to the opinions of men.

- Do not believe the lies of the devil.

- Do not look at the storms—only the Savior.

- Guard what your ears hear.

- Speak words of faith rooted in the Word.

Principle 4: Prepare for rain.

Remember how Elijah prepared? He prayed *expecting* rain. He sent his servant to look for rain. And as soon as the smallest evidence appeared that there would be rain—a little cloud on the horizon—Elijah immediately told King Ahab to get off the mountain and to the city because a great flood was coming.

Years later, Elijah's successor, Elisha, warned King Jehoshaphat to prepare for rain saying,

> Thus saith the Lord, Make this valley full of ditches. For thus saith the Lord, Ye shall not see wind, neither shall ye see rain; yet that valley shall be filled with water, that ye may drink, both ye, and your cattle, and your beasts.
>
> —2 Kings 3:16–17

When God promises rain, then get ready. Even when the kings of Israel did not see rain coming, they were told to get ready by the man of God. You must prepare for rain—the outpouring of God's Spirit and blessing—even when you cannot see it in the natural.

Prepare for rain even when there's not a cloud in the sky. Prepare for rain even when you feel nothing but doubt. Prepare for rain even when the stench of dryness and death is surrounding you. Your crops may be wasted in the field. Dust storms may be filling your nostrils. Arid winds may be cracking your lips and parching your soul. Nonetheless, *prepare for rain!*

Principle 5: Never take "No" for an answer.

Victory belongs to those who will not take "No" for an answer. Why? Because the promises of God in Christ are:

> . . . yea, and in him, Amen, unto the glory of God by us. Now he who stablisheth us with you in Christ, and hath anointed us, is God. Who hath also sealed us, and given the earnest of the Spirit in our hearts.
>
> —1 Corinthians 1:20–22

Elijah's servant had returned to him six times with the observation, "There is nothing" (1 Kings 18:43). But Elijah refused to take "No" for an answer. He continued in prayer on his knees with his face buried between his legs. What was happening? Simply this: When faith faces a lack of evidence, it refuses to allow the report to be final. No cloud was yet on the horizon. No immediate evidence in the natural existed to confirm the promised harvest from God. What must we do when faced with a lack of evidence? Refuse to accept "No" as the final answer and don't be afraid to look again. God has already said, "Yes." He has given His Word. Nothing else is needed to believe. We must hold on to God's Word even when evidence is lacking and all the signs fail.

Faith has two hinges. According to Romans 10:19, we believe in our hearts and then confess with our mouths. So Elijah's faith continued to confess that rain was coming. He prayed and believed in his heart that God would send the rain. He had heard God's Word, and so he believed. "So then faith cometh by hearing; and hearing by the word of God" (Rom. 10:17).

Elijah could not predict rain based on the conditions he saw in the natural. Famine and dryness filled the land. The hard, rocky soil was fallow. The crops were scarce. The curse of God was on the land, and no one praised His name. Yet after the defeat of Baal's prophets, even before he prayed, Elijah told Ahab, "Get thee up, eat and drink; for there is a sound of abundance of rain" (1 Kings 18:42).

There was not just an expected dew fall or shower. It was not just a shower or brief rain storm. Rather, rain was coming in abundance—a flood was on its way! No one else believed Elijah. No evidence or sign existed to verify that the rain was coming. And when the servant went to look, he pronounced the opinion of the majority of weather forecasters: "There is nothing."

Have you ever been there? Has famine, dry season, and lack of provision ever haunted your life? But you refused to believe the world's report. You rejected the majority opinion. You started believing in your heart and confessing with your mouth, *No More Crumbs!* Everyone around you thinks you are crazy. And you begin sowing in the midst of your famine—money, time, prayer, service, and praise. You sow even when your checkbook, your spouse, your mind and body all shout, "There is nothing!"

But long after everyone else has given up, you continue to persevere. You hold on to God's Word. You bake the last cake like the widow did. Like Elijah, you confess rain when there is no evidence of rain. Like Peter, you walk on water when walking on water is impossible. Like the woman with the issue of blood, you get down on your knees, humbling yourself, and crawl through the crowd to touch the hem of Jesus' garment. And then it comes. The promise is fulfilled. A tiny cloud is all it takes to stir hope within you. The rain begins to fall. The dry season is over. Finally, the harvest appears and there are *No More Crumbs!*

HOW DO WE HARVEST?

WE HAVE A PROBLEM as Christians. We are not putting our hand to the sickle and immediately harvesting. We are not as active in the harvest as we are in the sowing. And harvest time is the shortest period of time. It may take some time to plant seeds and wait for them to germinate. But when the fruit comes, we must immediately take up the sickle and bring in the harvest before it rots in the field.

God has brought forth a great harvest, but we have destroyed some of the crops, not knowing when or how to harvest. God did not say the harvest would just be translated from the field to our barns so that we might feast at a banquet table instead of eating crumbs. We must go get it. Let me share with you how to harvest:

Send forth holy angels.

We have the authority to send forth ministering spirits into the harvest.

But to which of the angels said he at any time, Sit on my right hand, until I make thine enemies thy footstool? Are they not all ministering spirits, sent forth to minister for them who shall be heirs of salvation?

—Hebrews 1:13

How do we reap? We speak the Word with authority. Jesus said to the Roman centurion, "I have not seen so great of faith in all of Israel." Why did He say that? Because the centurion said, "For I am a man under authority. And I say to this man, Go, and he goes. And I say to this man, Come hither, and he cometh." (Read Matthew 8:1–10.)

When was the last time you exercised your authority in faith and brought in your harvest? Isaiah 55:10 declares, "So shall my word be that goeth forth out of my mouth: it shall not return unto me void, but it shall accomplish that which I please, and it shall prosper in the thing whereto I sent it." And Proverbs 18:21 reveals, "Death and life are in the power of the tongue: and they that love it shall eat the fruit thereof." When was the last time that you spent time declaring God's Word of provision, perpetual privilege, and promised harvest in your life? When was the last time you sent forth ministering spirits into the harvest to get what belongs to you?

Psalm 103:20 declares, "Bless the Lord, ye his angels, that excel in strength, that do his commandments, hearkening unto the voice of his word." When the Word of the Lord goes forth—the written, prophetic or proclaimed Word—you must decide immediately whether you will speak and walk in His word or ignore it. At the moment of His Word, the Spirit discerns the intentions of your heart.

God knows if you are going through the rigors of religiosity or if you are committed by faith and prayer to move out into the harvest.

This should be the declaration of your mouth:

I send forth the holy angels of God right now.
They are commissioned to minister on behalf of the
heirs of salvation.

I am an heir of salvation.
I am washed in the blood of Christ.
I am blood-bought, Holy Ghost-filled, and fire-baptized.

I am not waiting to get into the kingdom of God.
I am in the kingdom now, and the kingdom is in me.
The King has come to live in me.
I have stepped out of darkness into light.
I have been translated from the kingdom of darkness
into the kingdom of light.
The love of God has been shed abroad in my heart
by Christ Jesus.

I have the covenant right that empowers me to
stand firm and to prophesy.
I have the covenant right to declare the holy angels of God
to go forth in the fields and bring in my harvest.
In the name and authority of Jesus. Amen.

Every day you can declare under the anointing of the Holy Spirit, "In the power of the Spirit and under the authority and inspiration of the Word, I declare that the holy angels go forth now and become reapers in the fields that I have sown which are white unto harvest." Do not wait until tomorrow to begin your declaration. Go forth and declare your harvest today and say, "I bind every hindering spirit on my life. I release the anointing of God with His angelic hosts to bring in my harvest."

Do not sit around like the Maytag repairman. Stop sitting around looking for someone to call and waiting for something to do. Stop watching your harvest rot in the field. Go get the harvest. Send forth ministering angels.

Prophesy your promised harvest.

I have already hinted at this second way to bring in the harvest. First, in the authority of your perpetual privilege as a child of God, send forth ministering angels into the promised harvest. Secondly, speak the Word. The Word will not return void. Fruit is borne when you speak life and not death. The testimony of Jesus is the spirit of prophecy. You stand and begin to declare your promised harvest. You begin to say things like,

- "The Word that God spoke to His Son is now spoken to me because I am in Christ" [2 Cor. 5:17].

- "I sit with Christ in heavenly places" [Eph. 2:6].

- "His Word abides mightily in me because I am His child" [1 Pet. 1:23; 1 John 2:14].

- "I am an heir and joint heir with Christ" [Rom. 8:17].

When you declare God's Word over what you have sown, you will find your fields white with harvest. For example, when the seed of the Word of God went into the borrowed tomb of Joseph of Arimathaea, the seed had life in itself. And through His servant David, God spoke His Word over the seed hundreds of years before the harvest. "For thou will not leave my soul in hell, neither wilt thou suffer thine Holy One to see corruption" (Ps. 16:10).

I am talking about resurrection seed. Are you ready to harvest? You cannot reap the promised harvest until you act with authority and sow seed. The seed that you sow in obedience to God's Word has life in it. Though it dies in the ground, it will spring forth as a harvest.

The promised harvest awaits you. Set aside your fear. Receive the peace of God so that you can prepare the field into which you are sowing. Like Mephibosheth, claim your rightful position as a child of God, as one with authority both to sow and reap. Begin sowing seed. Sow words of righteousness, encouragement, comfort, joy, and life into others. Sow financial seed into your church and ministries that advance the kingdom of God. Sow the seed of your time to witness to others and serve them in the name of Christ. Send forth ministering angels to bring in your harvest. And prophesy your promised harvest. Get ready to move into the abundant life of God's kingdom where lack becomes plenty, fear fades into confidence, and reaping rapidly follows sowing. As you sow, declare with your mouth and believe in your heart:

No More Crumbs!

5

A View from the Pigpen

ZAGAH, whose name means "wanderer," hungrily studied the husk, carefully examining the partially eaten ear of corn for any remaining kernel that he might pluck out for himself. His routine was well rehearsed. Each evening after slopping the pigs and making certain each had eaten its fill of corn, he gathered the gnawed husks together in a filthy, torn rag and carried them as precious jewels back to the corner of his mud hut on the edge of the pigpen.

Zagah's job was tending and feeding the unclean swine belonging to his pagan, Gentile lord. As dirty and humiliating as his job was, Zagah felt lucky to have a job. Months before, he had reached the end of a long string of parties and friends who had helped him squander his inheritance. Having lost everything, he looked around for any job that might put food in his stomach and a roof over his head. All his Jewish friends had abandoned him, believing Zagah's poverty to be a spiritual curse from God. His material lack, they believed, proved that God was punishing him for some hidden or unconfessed sin. None of his own countrymen would hire him, believing he was cursed. Only a heathen Gentile took pity on him and offered him a job tending what every self-respecting Jew knew to be unclean—pigs! Yes, he had been born a Jew. But certainly he had no home now.

More than a year ago, young Zagah had demanded his inheritance from his father. Surely by now his father had disowned him and pronounced him dead. *I have nothing to go back to*, he thought bitterly as he spied a solitary kernel buried in the midst of a layer of mud. Gingerly, he picked the uneaten kernel that the old sow had missed. Washing the kernel, he placed it in the center of his tongue and savored what had become his only hedge against starvation—eating the leftover husks of pigs.

What circumstances had brought this Jewish boy to such a humiliating and degrading position in life? He had been born into a prosperous and elite family. Certainly his inheritance would have been more than ample to provide for him into the twilight years of life. So what tragedy had tripped him up and landed him in a mud pit, tending pagan pork?

Zagah pondered his fate while his thoughts drifted to happier, bygone days.

HIS LONG SOJOURN had started back home outside of Tiberius, where Zagah's father owned a large estate built over the decades by his forefathers who tended sheep and pastured a few cattle. They had grown their own crops in the rich soil of the Galilee. Zagah possessed everything except the inheritance of the firstborn son. For years he had seethed inside with anger and jealousy. His older brother had it all—the lion's share of the inheritance, the honor of the firstborn, and the privileged seat at his father's table on the father's right hand. The arrogance of his older brother, who constantly rubbed his nose into his secondary status, filled Zagah with an desire to run away. Though his father had shown unconditional love to both boys, Zagah still felt left out, inferior, and like a piece of excess furniture in a crowded room.

Suddenly, a new idea came to him. No longer would he settle for the crumbs. He would get all that was due him right away. No longer would his brother dominate his life. No longer would he be number two. Now he would leave home and start a new life for himself in which he could be and do whatever he liked. No big brother would be looking over his shoulder. No father would be there to order him around and to discipline him. Life would be a party!

ZAGAH FINISHED his light meal of corn kernels and settled uneasily up against the mud wall of his hut. He hated the odor of hogs that permeated his clothes, skin, and hair. *What a life! Party's over*, he thought. In fact, life seemed to be over.

As exhaustion overtook him and restless sleep clouded his mind, he half-remembered and half-dreamed about his home, his father, and even his tormenting elder brother.

FOR WEEKS, Zagah had endlessly rehearsed in his mind the demand he would put to his father. *Father, I have no future here. Ezra has everything—the birthright, the main portion of the inheritance, and the honor of being your eldest son. I need a change of environment. Release me to go to another town and start a new life. Give me whatever share of the inheritance that would come to me. The money will make it possible for me to have a fresh start where no one knows me or you.*

He dreaded the look that he knew would come into his father's eyes. He knew his father loved him. But mere love wasn't enough for a prosperous life. Zagah needed money and a fresh start. Only leaving home could give him a future.

Finally, he had built up enough courage to approach his father. Ezra had gone into town, and all of the servants were out in the fields. As Zagah slipped into the house for a noon-day meal with his father, he began to tremble. Lips quivering, he recited his rehearsed speech in a trembling voice, staring at his feet because he could not bear to look into his father's eyes.

The few moments of silence that blanketed the room after his announcement seemed like an eternity. Zagah felt his father draw near. The old man's hands gingerly cradled Zagah's face and lifted his countenance so that the eyes of both men stared into one another's souls. His father's sad, grieving eyes gushed fountains of tears which poured down his father's bearded face and onto his own. Zagah felt a blush burn his cheeks as he too began to weep. Never had he seen such love and anguish in his father's eyes.

"My son, my son," moaned his father. "How I love you. What have I done to cause you to pronounce me dead in your own heart? Only my death could bring you your portion of the inheritance. Yet, while I still live, you ask for what could only be yours upon my death. Am I so meaningless to you that you no longer value me, but only my money and property?"

"No, Father, it is not that. But I feel so worthless and useless here. I am suffocating here under Ezra's heavy hand. I must leave and start a new life elsewhere. But my only hope for a new start is my inheritance so that I will have something for a new beginning."

"But your inheritance is secure. Your brother cannot touch anything that belongs to you. A third is yours by Torah. But as long as you are here, all the benefits of my estate are yours to enjoy now. Besides, I would rather die than to be separated from you," protested the father.

Barely able to speak through his sobs, Zagah mumbled his

broken response, "I know, Father, that you love me. I do love you. But I must go. Please do not make me stay. I can't breathe here. I must go."

"But where will you go?" asked the father.

"Parthia. Many Jews still live there because their fathers did not return with Nehemiah from the exile. And remember Rueben? When he moved there with his family last year, he promised I could come and live with him if I ever left home. His family prospers in trading with the caravans that come from the East. I will be fine. But I must have money to travel and to start over on my own," Zagah explained.

Reluctantly, Zagah's father agreed. He sold enough of his flocks to convert the son's portion of the inheritance to currency. And all too soon from his perspective, the day of departure came. As he handed Zagah the purse filled with gold talents, the father began to weep uncontrollably. He grabbed Zagah, embraced him, and kissed him on both cheeks.

"I will never give you up as dead, my son," the father promised. "Every day I will pray and wait for you on this path. I know—Jehovah as my witness—that someday He will bring you back to me." Without another look, his father rushed back inside the house while Zagah began his long journey to Dura-Europus on the banks of the mighty Euphrates.

Never again will I walk this road. Never again will I have to hear my brother's jibes. Never again will I sweat in the fields caring for cattle and sheep. Today I am free, never again to work against my will, Zagah thought gleefully.

ZAGAH'S JOURNEY east to Parthia was exciting, but expensive. A caravan of Indian traders allowed Zagah to ride on camels with them to Dura, but the cost emptied his purse of a third of his talents. *Well worth the cost to travel such a long distance and have food to eat,* he reasoned. His heart pounded on the day he first saw Dura gleaming in the distance. The alabaster buildings and the impressive towers catching the last fleeting rays of the sunset inspired awe in the young Galilean. Never had he seen such splendor and wealth.

The caravan entered the city gates just as darkness covered the city and hundreds of twinkling lights came on through countless windows. Torches lit the streets, and the marketplace still thronged with traders bartering with locals over everything from exotic silks to oriental spices. As the caravan deposited Zagah in the middle of the marketplace and wound its way back into the city's environs, Zagah wandered aimlessly through the massive market, excited by all the new sights and smells.

Soon his pack grew heavy on his shoulders and his stomach began to growl for dinner. Buying a small meat pie from the closest vendor, he moved to a quiet corner up against the wall and sat down to feast his lips on a new, tasty morsel while feasting his eyes on sights he had never seen before. *What a great place to start over,* he mused.

He continued to reflect, *Leaving home wasn't all that hard. After father's tears and a few dusty miles down the road, the past is already dead and forgotten. Listening to the Indian traders tell mysterious tales of the Far East was fascinating. And now here I am. A new home with new adventures. Being out of control and away from home is really exciting. Life doesn't get any better than this. Soon I will have new friends, a new business, and a new way of life. No more crumbs for me. I can make it big on my own! So long, brother. Good riddance!*

Before long, Zagah began to make his way through the market, asking everyone who understood Aramaic where he might find the house of Joshua, the father of Rueben.

"Ah, you mean the Galilean," responded one woman arranging the fruit in her cart. "Want some figs?" she asked hoping to make one last sale before turning in for the night.

"Sure," responded Zagah. As he reached for a denarius, he asked again, "What about Joshua, the Galilean? Do you know where he lives?"

"Of course!" she answered grabbing the denarius and thrusting a cluster of ripe figs into his hand. "He and his family come to the market regularly and buy some of my fruit. Go two streets down and turn to your left. His house is the fifth one along the brick way. You cannot miss it." And off she rushed into the night.

Zagah made his way to the brick street and counted the houses on the way until he stood before a simple stone dwelling with a heavy wooden door. Taking a deep breath, he knocked firmly and then waited for a reply. No answer. Again he knocked but this time louder and harder. After a few moments a slot about chest high opened in the door and an eye peered at Zagah. "Oh, dear God," exclaimed the familiar voice on the other side of the door. "It's Zagah!"

Suddenly the door flew wide open and Rueben rushed headlong into Zagah's arms. Both childhood buddies hugged and laughed as they danced joyfully together. Rueben gathered up Zagah's bag and pushed him into a long corridor toward the center of the house. Both laughing friends stumbled together into a large atrium where a half dozen young men and women were drinking, talking loudly, and creating a carousing uproar.

Zagah regained his composure and steadied himself against the closest wall while Rueben rushed to a nearby waterpot and poured a fresh drink for his reunited companion. Slowly Zagah's eyes adjusted to the occupants of the dimly lit room. A few couples had paired off and were embracing one another passionately. Others were shouting at one another while consuming one chalice after another of the waterpot's spirits. Parched from his journey, Zagah gulped down his cup's contents. His tongue tingled with delight. Never before had he tasted such sweet and flowery wine. It was so light and enchanting that no sooner than he finished one cup, he reached for another.

Rueben saw to it that Zagah's bag was carted off to a vacant room. "My parents are gone for the fortnight," Rueben exclaimed. "The house, the wine, and the food here are all ours. Enjoy yourself."

For hours Zagah and Rueben talked about old times. After many chalices of new wine, Zagah found his conversation drifting away like random notes in an unchained melody. Unaccustomed to so much drink, he slumped on his couch and drifted into a drunken stupor, not to awaken until the next afternoon.

LIVING WITH RUEBEN was an endless party. Zagah got caught up in the fast life and easy women of the city. Soon forgotten were his aspirations to start a new business and a new life. The more he partied, gambled, and spent on his new friends, the more new friends he had. For months, day and night melted into one another as Zagah slid from orgy to orgy and woman to woman. Everyone loved him and freely spent his energy and his money.

Almost forgotten were the starlit nights on Galilean hills where Zagah had kept his father's flocks, stroked a lyre, and sung ancient psalms written by a shepherd king who had lived centuries earlier. Life had become too much fun to think about home, old traditions, family, and a routine existence. Zagah's life throbbed with every sensual pleasure he could imagine, and some of which he could never have imagined. But slowly, as a cistern with a pinhole leak ebbing out its precious water, Zagah's inheritance drained away into wanton excursions whose only lasting power was a lingering addiction for more and more—sex, wine, partying, and wild living.

No sooner than Zagah's purse emptied and his luck failed was the advent of the worst summer drought ever to hit the region. Crops wasted in the field as the scorching sun dried the countryside into endless dunes of shifting desert sand. Hot southerly winds blew across the land with no moisture in sight. Cloudless skies yielded weeks devoid of moisture. A dry season engulfed the land, and even many of Dura's wealthy citizens became destitute and desperate. For their last bags of flour and meager provisions for a journey, Rueben's family sold everything, deciding to return to their homeland, the hills of Galilee.

But not Zagah! He had lost everything but his pride. He wandered through the deserted marketplace. Where carts and wagons overflowing with produce had been parked just months before, now the brick streets were empty, save for a few wandering orphans driven out by starving families seeking to survive by ridding themselves of helpless, hungry children too young to work or to beg. With bloated stomachs and gaunt faces, the emaciated children wandered Dura's empty streets searching for just a crumb to eat. But there were no crumbs to be found, and dozens of tiny bodies littered the streets.

Zagah, gagging and nauseated by the stench of death everywhere, fled the city for the countryside downriver. Finally he stumbled upon a hog farm whose rancid smells rivaled the city's putrid odors. On the edge of starvation, Zagah sold himself to the hogs' owner for the meager wages of eating the hogs' cornhusks in exchange for daily cleaning the pigpens.

For one who was determined never to work hard again, the labor was both hard and endless. Barely surviving on the few kernels of corn he could find in each grazed-upon husk, Zagah slopped the pigs and began to think once again of a homestead where even the servants had a better life than he did.

Each night he fell exhausted into the corner of his hut. His dreams haunted him with scenes of clean clothes and tables laden with food. Such were the dreams of childhood years now long departed. And each dream seemed to have the same ending. Zagah would see himself crawling under a lavishly spread banquet table searching desperately for the crumbs that might have fallen onto the floor. Just eating the crumbs from his father's table was a better existence than anything he could hope for in a foreign land. So he dreamed. But his dreams could never satisfy his craving stomach or empty soul.

THAT FATEFUL DAY in Zagah's life started like the previous stream of empty days and fitful nights. Aching in every muscle of his body with every cell crying out for food, Zagah wearily stacked the wiry ears of corn on a wooden cart and made his way once again to the pigpens. The hogs sounded their bottomless cravings with loud snorts as Zagah approached their pens.

Then, Zagah froze behind his cart with eyes fixed on the horizon. From the east a caravan slowly began to appear. Something was vaguely familiar about the banners flying over the lead camels. He had seen those identifying colors before. Suddenly his heart stopped and his stomach leapt into his throat.

The caravan . . . the camels . . . the banners . . . they look just like the traders who brought me here from Galilee.

Dropping the cart handles, Zagah began to walk, then jog, and finally sprint toward the caravan. As he raced toward the approaching gaggle of traders, thoughts that were unthinkable just minutes before began to explode in his brain.

I can go home. Father promised to wait and pray for me. I will ask his forgiveness. I will even be his servant. Even his servants have it better than most free men here. Just eating the crumbs off his table will be enough for me. I can cope with Ezra. His taunting doesn't begin to compare with starvation. I will return home!

The harder he ran toward the Indian caravan, the more the fog that had clouded his brain began to clear. Yes, he was the son of a wealthy land owner. Yes, he did have an inheritance—not material goods, but a relationship. Yes, there was a place for him to live and a bed to sleep in. Yes, he had been the fool. But now, it was all so clear. He would beg his father's forgiveness, confess his sin, and ask to be just a servant—not a son.

Yes, he did have an inheritance—not material goods, but a relationship.

The approaching traders barely recognized the fat, well dressed boy they had dropped off at Dura less than a year before. A gaunt, emaciated skeleton now rushed to the caravan's leader shouting his name and begging for mercy. Could this be the same arrogant kid that they had conned out of so much gold? Surely not. But certainly it was.

Throwing himself at the feet of Akbar, the caravan's owner, Zagah begged for mercy. Akbar was in a great mood. His caravan was loaded with oriental silks and spices. He knew this would be the most profitable trip ever. Why not help a broken kid who had been humbled into manhood in the fiery crucible of suffering and pain? Like the blacksmith's hammer pounds molten iron into a usable shape, so the fire of Yahweh's law of sowing and reaping had shaped Zagah into a vessel that could now receive grace and instruction. Besides, Akbar needed someone to water and clean up after the camels. What a fitting job for the former fat boy who thought he had the world on a string. Laughing to himself, Akbar motioned to the slaves to throw Zagah across a donkey and bring him along at the rear of the procession across the desert to Galilee.

FOR WEEKS, Zagah tended the caravan's camels without so much as a fleeting protest. Humbly he obeyed Akbar's every command or whimsical notion. All those in the caravan who remembered Zagah from his previous journey marveled at the change in his appearance and attitude. Stripped down to a loin cloth and thoroughly scrubbed at the first oasis—a one night's journey from Dura—Zagah now glistened with sweat beading on a bronzed body devoid of fat as he tended the camels and obeyed Akbar's every command.

Secretly Akbar wondered if Zagah's family would take the runaway wanderer back. He hoped that they would not just so that he could keep this productive, new servant. Yet something in Akbar's heart told him that once the caravan passed by Galilee, this hungry castaway would find a welcome reception back home.

As the caravan crossed the Jordan close to its Gennesaret headwaters, Zagah began to worry and toss restlessly in his sleep. Once again he dreamed of crawling under his father's table and looking for crumbs. Demons tormented his mind, assuring him that his father would angrily throw him from the house and send him wandering the rest of his life:

You will never be forgiven. You deserve nothing but condemnation. Your father has already pronounced you dead. Too much pain has been inflicted. By now, your father has fully sided with your brother and rejected you as not only an heir but even as a slave. So the torturous thoughts pounded in his head as the caravan snaked closer and closer to his homestead.

Nonetheless, the day came when the caravan was less than a day's journey by foot to Zagah's home. Taking leave of his Indian master, he promised never to forget his kindness and mercy. Akbar shrugged. The exorbitant fee he had exacted from Zagah on the first leg of his sojourn had more than paid for ten such round trips. Besides, he had gotten a free servant for his camel on the return trek. In every respect, Akbar had profited from the foolish Galilean.

With nothing left but a broken and contrite heart, Zagah made his way through fields and pastures he had played in throughout his childhood. He was first overwhelmed by nostalgia, then by torrents of shame and guilt.

What a fool I have been! thought Zagah. *If I see my father, I will fall at his feet and repent. I will ask him to forgive me and make me his lowliest servant. Just to sweep his floor and eat his crumbs will be enough for me. How I have sinned against God Almighty and my father!*

One more hill remained between Zagah and the last stretch of rocky path leading up to his father's house. His mind raced with thoughts cascading through his conscious-ness like hundreds of waterfalls. *Will he be there? Will he even know me? What if he hates me? I have nothing to offer him but my brokenness. Everyone will laugh at me. What shame I have brought upon myself and my family! Perhaps I should have just died in a foreign land. Unnoticed. Destitute. Worthless. Forgotten. I haven't forgotten anything about my father—his eyes, his tears, his parting words. If only he would let me eat the crumbs—that would be enough!*

A FEW MORE STEPS and Zagah would crest the hill. His future was beyond his reach. His destiny was out of his hands. His squandered inheritance could not be earned back, even by a lifetime of hard work and slave labor. He was noth-ing and had nothing. Nothing, that is, except a promise. Was a promise enough to cross over from his shattered past into a new life? He had once run away from a promise, hoping to find a new life. Now he knew in the depths of his soul that the only life he would ever have depended on a father's promise. Would that promise be enough to start over again?

6

The Great Homecoming

J UST BEFORE he crested the last hill on his way home, Zagah stopped in his tracks. *What if my father isn't there, and I must first face Ezra? What if Father has completely disowned me as if I was dead? What if he's angry with me and won't forgive me? What if I say the wrong thing? What if . . .?*

The *what if's* in life are the last stumbling blocks that Satan puts in our path in order to rob us of our inheritance. *What if's* always keep us focused on fear, not faith. *What if's* continually distract us from our vision. *What if's* turn us away from possibilities to problems, from positives to negatives, and from hope to despair. The last hurdle that Zagah had to overcome was *what if.*

Just before the hill is crested and the problem is solved, just before the impossible becomes possible and the harvest is reaped, we are tempted to pause and dwell in the morass of *what if.* The longer we stall, the higher the mountain seems, the greater the problem appears, and the longer we must wait for our answer. How many inheritances have been lost by those who chose not to finish strong and not to hold on to the promise to the end?

Zagah had gone through too much, lost too much, and traveled too far to stop now. And he knew it. The crest of the hill rose before him. The end of the journey was within sight. The father's promise lay on the other side of his doubt and fear. Now was the time to finish the journey he had started months ago. Now was the time to face his father and repent. Now was the time to confront any consequences that awaited him. Closing his eyes and feeling his heart pound in his temples, Zagah took the final steps to crest the hill and bring his home into view.

Before his eyes opened, tears began streaming down his cheeks. Overwhelming shame and guilt flooded his soul.

From his broken heart freely flowed cleansing torrents of repentance. Through the blurring downpour of tears, Zagah opened his eyes and strained to see home for the first time after what seemed like an eternity of separation. In the distance he first spied the familiar estate with its fields of ripening crops and vineyards.

Slowly his eyes cleared, and then he saw for the first time a solitary figure standing by the front gate. Immediately he knew it was his father. Without hesitation, Zagah's walk turned into a jog and then a sprint as he dropped everything and lunged forward. With every muscle in his body aching and straining to the limit like a great sprinter in an Olympic dash for the finish line, he ran toward his home. But the distance to the front gate was halved by another sprinter— his father. Rushing headlong toward his son, the father actually covered the distance between them much faster than his son.

The father grabbed his son's shoulders, kissed his cheeks, and hugged his boy so hard that he squeezed the air out of his lungs. Freeing himself from his father's embrace, Zagah fell to his knees sobbing uncontrollably and gasped, "Father, I have sinned against heaven and you. I am no longer worthy to be called your son. . . ."

Interrupting his speech, the father sobbed, "My son, my son. I thought you were dead, but Jehovah, blessed be His Name, in His mercy has answered my prayers and brought you back from the dead."

Hearing the commotion outside the gate, the servants of the household had assembled in front of the house to witness this miraculous reunion. Not one of them had a dry eye.

Issuing a joyous command, the father shouted, "Get me my best robe. Find my signet ring and my sandals. Hurry! My son is half naked, and I must clothe him. Kill the fatted calf we have been preparing for the holy days. Today is holy. For this, my son, was dead and is alive again; he was lost, and is found. We must all celebrate with a feast tonight!"

Astonished and speechless, Zagah began to weep again as he collapsed in a shaking, sobbing heap before his father. One servant rushed to the reunited pair with a robe and perfume. Promptly the father stripped the rags from his boy's body, anointed him with perfume, and draped his best robe about Zagah's broad shoulders. Then he reached for his ring and pushed it on Zagah's finger. Finally putting his arms around Zagah's waist, the father literally carried his boy into the house as servants frantically rushed in every direction, preparing for a great feast.

UNAWARE OF the day's events, Zagah's older brother, Ezra, made his way in from the fields toward the house. Weary to the bone, he plodded slowly and boiled with resentment. *That worthless leech of a brother*, he thought. *First he steals from my father the inheritance that was not due him for years. Then he breaks my father's heart and runs away. Now I am left with everything. I do my work and his. Father leans on me for everything while he goes and sits at the gate every day praying for sluggard Zagah to come back home. What a waste! Surely Zagah is dead by now from drinking and partying. He probably ended*

*up dying in a drunken stupor in some foreign ditch and was eaten
by stray dogs. Such a fate he deserved! But I never deserved this.
I do the work of three men and Father never so much as says,
"Thank you." No one appreciates me. I'm tired, dirty, and fed up
with this work. Tonight, I will have a talk with Father and confront him with reality. Zagah is dead, and it's time for him to face
the truth and get on with his life.*

As Ezra rounded the last curve in the rocky path leading up
to the house, he stopped with open-mouthed surprise. Instead
of the normal, quiet atmosphere that settled at dusk over the
estate, a blazing fire barbecued a calf behind the house. Loud
music echoed through the glen. Servants were rushing everywhere like ants preparing for a feast. Some were even dancing to
the music. *What in heaven's name is happening?* Ezra wondered.

As he approached a handmaid rushing toward the well
with pot on her head, Ezra stopped her and impatiently
asked, "What's happening? What's with all the music and
dancing? Has a special guest unexpectedly arrived from
Jerusalem?" All Ezra could imagine was that his father's
brother—Joshua, a Levite from the Temple in the city of
David—could have arrived for a surprise visit.

"No, master," the girl replied trying to conceal her delight,
knowing the animosity between the two brothers. "Zagah has
returned. Our lord has pronounced a feast. Everyone is cele-
brating and making ready."

Ezra began to tremble in anger and disbelief. The worst
thing he could have imagined had happened. Despicable
Zagah had returned. As bad as life had been without him
around, now things were even worse. Instead of rebuking and

disciplining Zagah, Father had done the unthinkable. He had forgiven him and was now making a fool of himself by throwing a party for the black sheep of the family. *Cursed be this house*, exploded Ezra's thoughts. *First my brother brought shame upon our family name, and now my father acts the fool with this stupid celebration!*

As the handmaid rushed back into the house with her full pot balanced carefully on her head, Ezra slumped down and sat on the rocky rim of the well. Sullen and smoldering with anger and hatred, he sat there sulking as the strains of joyful psalms filled the evening air.

AS THE HANDMAID HURRIED toward the banquet room, the father noticed her pot of water and asked, "Did you see Ezra returning from the fields when you were at the well?"

"Yes, my lord."

"Does he know his brother is alive and returned home? Is he on his way into the house?" inquired the father.

"My lord, I told him about his brother. But when I spoke, he became angry. I last saw him sitting by the well," she replied.

Immediately the father left the party and rushed toward the well. He knew his sons well. *Ezra will be upset*, he thought. *But he must come and welcome his brother. This is a day of rejoicing . . . of forgiveness . . . of reconciliation. It's a new start for all of us.*

Ezra saw his father approaching and turned his back on him. Lovingly, his father came up behind Ezra and threw his arms around his neck. "Ezra, your brother has returned. He's safe and unharmed. God is so good. Please come rejoice with everyone."

Angrily, Ezra threw his father's arms off of his neck and got in his father's face. "What about me?" he protested. "I never stole my inheritance from you. I never rebelled. I have been by your side all these months and you never threw me a party. But as soon as Zagah—and he's always been your favorite—came running home after losing everything on harlots and gambling, you welcome him back as if nothing has happened. *Raca!* Both you and Zagah are fools! I'll have nothing to do with you or this party!"

Once again, the father's eyes filled with pain. First, it had been a younger son running away. But now, his dear firstborn, to whom he had entrusted everything, was turning against him. "Son, you have always been with me. All your inheritance

The son who had never known lack could not appreciate the abundance of his inheritance.

and all that I possess have always been yours. But today it is fitting to give thanks to the Lord. We are not rejoicing over Zagah's past mistakes. But he was dead, and now God has brought him back to us alive and well. He was lost but now is found!"

Shrugging off his father's entreaty, Ezra walked away filled with bitterness and resentment. The son who had never known lack could not appreciate the abundance of his inheritance.

Meanwhile, in the house a party continued. And the son who had known nothing but lack in his sojourn to a far country now sat at a banquet table fit for a king. Quietly, he whispered a blessing for the food: *Father God, I give You praise for reminding my father of his promise to me during my absence. I give You praise for Your provision, O God. As You spread this table before me, I declare: **No More Crumbs!***

FATHER, GIVE ME

AS MUCH AS WE HAVE CRITICIZED the younger son in Jesus' parable of the Loving Father (Luke 15:11–32), we need to see that Jesus never spoke an ill word or corrected the actions of the younger son. Jesus does not criticize him for asking the father for his inheritance. Of course, what the younger son does with the inheritance is sinful. But I want you to notice: God wants to give us what belongs to us.

> God wants to give us what belongs to us.

I did not say that God gives us what we deserve or earn. We do not have the right to demand anything of God. "For by grace are ye saved through faith; and that not of yourselves, it is the gift of God—not of works, lest any man should boast" (Eph. 2:8–8). The younger son had done nothing to earn his inheritance. It was a gift from his father.

Likewise, our inheritance from our heavenly Father is a gift. Consider the first chapter of Ephesians.

> Blessed be the God and Father of our Lord Jesus Christ, who hath blessed us with all spiritual blessings in heavenly places in Christ, According as he hath chosen us in him before the foundation of the world, that we should be holy and without blame before him, in love Having predestined us unto the adoption of children by Jesus Christ to himself, according to the good pleasure of his will . . . In whom [Christ] also we have obtained an inheritance, being predestinated according to the purpose of him who worketh all things after the counsel of his own will.
>
> —Ephesians 1:3–6, 11

In Christ, God chose us, we didn't choose Him. God blessed us. God made us holy and blameless through the shed blood of Jesus. God predestined us to be His children. God gave us an inheritance in Christ Jesus. Like that younger son, everyone trusting Jesus is God's child, saved and adopted by Him. As His children, we have obtained His inheritance for us.

So when the younger son requested, "Father, give me the portion of good that falleth to me [my inheritance]," the father had no reservation in giving his son what already belonged to him.

Why is it that we are settling for the crumbs of life instead of life itself? Why is it that as God's children we are content with crumbs instead of an abundant banquet filled with all that God wants us to have? The answer is simple. The Word

111

declares, "You have not, because you ask not" (James 4:2). Nowhere in Scripture will you find God not answering prayer. God always answers our prayers. "Therefore, I say unto you, whatever things ye desire, when ye pray, believe that ye receive them, and ye shall have them" (Mark 11:24). He delights to give us what we ask of Him.

The father in this parable is like our heavenly Father. When he is asked by the younger son for the inheritance that is his, the Father says, "Yes!" God's promises are always true. He promises:

> And this is the confidence that we have in him [God], that if we ask any thing according to his will, he heareth us; And if we know that he hears us, whatever we ask, we know that we have the petitions that we have desired of him.
>
> —1 John 5:14–15

The same God, who keeps His promises, declares through Jeremiah, "Call unto me and I will answer thee and I will show thee great and mighty things which thou knowest not" (Jer. 33:3). So we should not negatively judge the younger son for coming in and asking his father for what rightfully belongs to him as an heir. The inheritance was already his. If it had not already belonged to him, the father would never have given it to him.

There is no hesitation on the father's part. While he may have been sad to see his son depart, he never questioned his son's right to the inheritance.

BUT, WHAT IF?

STILL YOU MAY ASK, "But what if the father had known that his son was going to mess up and squander the inheritance? Would he still have given it?" Let me ask you, "Is our inheritance from God conditional or unconditional?" If any of us were saved from our sins by Christ based on the condition that once saved we would never sin again, then none of us would ever be saved. God does not say, "I promise to save you, if you will never sin again." Nor does He demand, "If I give you your inheritance, you must never make a mistake in how you use or spend it."

Certainly, the prodigal son's father could have guessed that his son was up to no good. Surely he was wise enough to discern that the embittered son would not sagely invest his inheritance. The father gave unconditionally just as he forgave unconditionally.

The covenant relationship that the father had with his children could not be broken by the mistakes and failures of his children. The father never said, "Son, you will have no more crumbs, if. . . ." You may temporarily lose your way, but you will not lose your relationship. You may fail and lose what you have had, but you will

You can lose everything you have, but you can never lose everything God has.

113

never lose what God has for you. Remember, the father gave the younger son all the portion that belonged to him. But, the story never says that the father gave the younger son everything that belonged to the father. The father's possessions were far greater than anything the son could ever possess or lose.

You may bankrupt yourself, but you can never bankrupt God. You can lose everything you have, but you can never lose everything God has. You can run away from God, but God will never run away from you. You can lose your love for yourself and God, but you can never make God stop loving you. God says to His children, "Yea, I have loved thee with an everlasting love; therefore, with loving-kindness have I drawn thee" (Jer. 31:3).

The fact that the younger son ran away didn't cause the father to stop loving him. The same is true in our relationship with God. David describes God's loving presence that abides with us in this way: "Whither shall I go from thy Spirit? Or whither shall I flee from thy presence? If I ascend up into heaven, thou art there; if I make my bed in hell, behold thou art there" (Ps. 139:8).

Think about these truths:

- God always answers the prayers of His children.

- God always gives us what we ask in His will.

- The inheritance given to us by God in Christ belongs to us now.

- A child may fail, mess up or run from the Father, but he can never hide from Him.

- God's inheritance for us is a gift—it cannot be earned or lost.

- His love for us is unconditional—nothing you do can make Him stop loving you.

WHAT ABOUT THE ELDER SON?

THE ELDER SON became angry because of the father's love and forgiveness toward his younger brother. He mistakenly believed that he had earned or deserved something from the father. So he lied to himself and his father: "Lo, these many years do I serve thee, neither transgressed I at any time thy commandment; and yet thou never gavest me a kid, that I might make merry with my friends" (Luke 15:29).

Wrong. This elder son had a big problem! He had developed an attitude of ingratitude and an outlook of lack. Look at what he thought and compare it with the truth:

The older son's lie	**The truth**
"I have served you."	He was being served.
"I have never sinned."	He was a sinner.
"You have never given me anything."	He had it all.
"I never had any fun."	He lacked joy.

"I have served you."

There is a big difference between being a slave and being a bondservant. God's children are bondservants, not slaves. We once were slaves to sin, but are now bondservants to Christ. A slave is an unwilling captive or prisoner who is forced to serve his master. But a bondservant is one who has been redeemed from the slavery of sin and freed to serve willingly in liberty and out of love for his master.

This older son has the wrong attitude toward serving his father. He serves out of duty and obligation. True servanthood is nothing like slavery and everything like waiting tables. Let me show you what I mean. A slave serves his master's table under compulsion and threat to his life. He would rather do anything in life than what he is doing.

However, a waiter serves his customer's table willingly. He wants the job. He enjoys the benefits. And his sole desire is to please the one whom he serves. He knows an inheritance is his. He understands that the one upon whom he waits pays the bills, keeps him in a job, and rewards him— the customer actually serves his needs by contributing to his salary and his tips. Now, no analogy is perfect. We can find places where this analogy doesn't fit and falls short of depicting our relationship with God. But taken on the surface, we

> True servanthood is nothing like slavery and everything like waiting tables.

can learn much about the difference between serving as a slave versus serving as a waiter.

Are you a slave or a waiter before God? Slaves always expect God to do something for them. They are always complaining about their work load and lack of adequate recognition. But waiters love just hanging out with the Lord. Being in His presence is reward enough for waiting upon Him. Their attitude is one of gratitude. Instead of always whining, they are always worshipping. They understand the paradoxes of servanthood:

- The servant is actually being served (Luke 12:37).

- The last is always first (Luke 22:26; Mark 10:43–45; Matt. 23:10–12).

- Those at the back of the table always go to the head of the table (Luke 14:8–10).

- Rewards are never earned but are always given (Matt. 20:1–16).

Jesus did not come to be served but to serve. You are not serving the Lord; He is serving you! He emphasized this truth with His disciples: "Henceforth I call you not servants; for the servant knoweth not what his lord doeth: but I have called you friends; for all things that I have heard of my Father I have made known unto you" (John 15:15).

> You are not serving the Lord; He is serving you!

Jesus is putting a towel around His waist. Bowing down, He kneels before you and washes your feet. He died for you. You are the vessel into which God pours His blessing. You are the recipient of His love. You are the conduit of His mercy. So who gave you a slave mentality? Not Christ. As a part of His beloved Church, you are His bride.

I married Joni in order to bless her. I did not marry her the first year we met because I only made a small amount every week. It was not enough income to take care of her, much less bless her. So I worked another year and still did not make enough. I thought, *She will never marry me and go down the ladder. When she marries me, I want her to climb the ladder and be inundated with my love.*

God seeks us out to love us, not to enslave us.

"For God so loved the world that he gave his only begotten Son" (John 3:16). Do you see both the purpose and object of His love? You and me. He purposed to create us so that He could lavish His love on us. God had no need for countless slaves working for Him. God desired you to be the object of His character—God is love (1 John 4:8). God seeks us out to love us, not to enslave us.

We have reversed His intention for us. We lie to ourselves and others when we say, "Oh, I'm serving the Lord." Impossible! He needs nothing from you. He is El Shaddai—the Self-Sufficient One. When you thought that you served Him, what did you do? Did you help Him breathe? Did you give Him strength? Did you offer Him advice? Did you plan His day? Of course not! "The steps of a good man are ordered by the Lord" (Ps. 37:23). He is the lover of your soul! Out of love for Him, you serve others. But do not miss this point: Out of love for you, He serves you!

"I have never sinned."

The elder son believed and lived a lie all the time he stayed at home. Yes, the younger son lived a lie when he ran away from home. But the elder son was just as separated from the father as the younger son. He actually believed that he served his father without sin. "If we say we have no sin, we deceive ourselves" (1 John 1:8). The younger son had been a physical vagabond running away to a foreign land, but the elder son had been a spiritual vagabond. While living under the same roof as his father, he had fled from the father's love. Instead of receiving grace and loving-kindness, he had attempted to earn approval through service.

> Too often we settle for the crumbs of slavery instead of feasting at His banquet table of love.

Too often we settle for the crumbs of slavery instead of feasting at His banquet table of love. When will we begin to understand that we are not sacrificing anything for Jesus? He laid down His life for us— not we for Him. He took the penalty of sin and guilt upon

Himself—not we for Him. He hung on the tree and died—not we for Him. Why? To lavish the Father's love upon us.

"You have never given me anything."

Even though the older son remained at home, he had missed out on his inheritance. The father reminds him that he could have eaten a fatted calf at any time. "And he [the father] said unto him, Son, thou art ever with me, and all that I have is thine" (Luke 15:30). Not some but *all* belonged to him. Not someday but *any* day. Not if his father loved him but *because* his father loved him. The Lord has spread the banquet table for you, and off you go into the kitchen trying to cook the meal just like Martha, instead of sitting at Jesus' feet like Mary (Luke 10:41–42).

"I never had any fun."

The older son could have been feasting at the table of his father's love. Instead, he was sweating hard in the fields, working him to the point of exhaustion, and trying to prove something to his father. Perhaps he was trying to prove that he was better than the younger son. Perhaps he was trying to prove that he could accomplish more in life than anyone else, including his father. Perhaps he was trying to prove that he deserved to be loved, affirmed, and accepted. Remember the harvest in Mark 4:26–29? A sower goes out to sow. He sows his seed into the ground and then sleeps and rises day and night. The seed then springs up, he knows not how. The earth bears fruit—first the blade, then the ear, and finally the full corn. And immediately when the fruit is come, the sower becomes the harvester, taking the sickle to the harvest. Why immediately? Because harvest time is the shortest time. Never let the harvest stay in the field too long. It will spoil. Go immediately to the harvest.

So it is with the inheritance of the Lord. The feast is ready. The table is spread. The fatted calf is prepared. You have nothing to prove to the Father! Don't clean yourself up (you couldn't even if you wanted to). Let Him cleanse you. Don't

Get out of the pigpen and start running toward the cross.

work day and night to earn the wages of salvation (the only wages you can earn are the wages of sin and death). Trust Him for the free gift of salvation. Come running down the road just like the younger son—dirty, tired, polluted, immoral, washed-up, failing, and desperate. Get out of the pigpen and start running toward the cross.

Get out from under the table where you are eating crumbs and run to the feast. One has been prepared in your honor without your effort. Grace has nothing to do with what you have done. His free gift awaits you. Come home to the Father!

THE FATHER IS LOOKING
FOR CHILDREN TO COME HOME

WHAT WAS THE FATHER DOING while his younger son was in a far country? First, let me tell you what he wasn't doing. He was not judging him. He was not criticizing or putting him down. He was not condemning him. The father was waiting for him. Understand this: The Father didn't create you to judge you but to love you.

The father waited and waited. Each day he patiently and hopefully looked down the path yearning to see his child returning home.

Search the Gospels. Nowhere will you find a person who was ever refused anything from Jesus. At times, He gave conditions to test the hearts of those who wanted something from him like the rich young ruler (Luke 19). Yes, he could have received the eternal life which he sought. But Jesus told him to first let go of his idol—money. Once he had sold everything and given it to the poor, he could follow Jesus and receive the abundant life he desired.

Jesus healed the leper, the blind man, the woman with the issue of blood, and the paralytic. He restored the man with the withered hand and raised Jarius' daughter and Lazarus from the dead. Why? Because Jesus was just like His Father. He was a giver and a lover. He was the Father with hands and feet. He was Word that became flesh and dwelt among us (John 1:14).

He wants us to live forever so that He can love us forever!

So God touched human life through a man—Jesus. He came not to be served but to serve. Like the father waiting for his prodigal son to come home, the Father waited for an eternity for us to come home, back into

His arms. After waiting and waiting, God could wait no more. Love seeks out that which is loved. Before we could ever turn back toward home, He came to us through His Son, Jesus. He gave us everything we asked for and more. Before we asked, He died for us, offering us His eternal gift of love—everlasting life. He wants us to live forever so that He can love us forever!

Like the prodigal son, we may run to the Father, fall at His feet, and beg to serve Him. He always refuses. Instead, He picks us up, bathes us with His tears, clothes us with a white robe of righteousness washed in the blood of Jesus, puts the ring of power and authority on our finger, and ushers us into a feast fit for the King.

Do not expect to sit under the table and hungrily grab for any crumb that may fall. No, in Christ you sit at the Father's right hand—the seat of honor. And to your surprise, when you reach out to fill His cup and serve His plate, His hand stops yours. In wonderment, you look into His eyes. All you want to do is to serve Him. Then you know the truth. He seats you at the King's table for one purpose—to serve *you*. Suddenly the reality of His dream for you is fulfilled:

No More Crumbs!

7

⁓

The Anointed One

ASA LOOKED on as the other children romped and
ran through the narrow streets of Capernaum.
Some played tag, freezing in position whenever
"it" got them. Asa had never been "it." Others used sticks to
hit a rounded stone past their opponents while everyone tried
to steal the stone and keep it way from the others as long as
possible. Asa had never hit the stone or played "keep away"
with the other children.

A gaggle of small children used an old rag as a blindfold.
The blindfolded child tried to catch those circled around
him and calling out his name. But Asa had never been

blindfolded. Each day was the same. After morning chores and studying the Torah, the children took to the streets to run, laugh, and play while Asa sat on a stone bench outside his house and watched all the others have fun without him. As the others played, he sat there in the warm, Galilean sun, daydreaming about what life might have been if he had been born normal.

Asa saw himself running and playing like the others. He dreamed of being normal, grabbing a stick with two strong hands and being the champion at stealing the round stones from the rest of the guys. After all, both of his legs were strong. In the evenings as the torrid sun set in the west, he would go out to the hillsides around the town and run in the dry, cool night. As he ran, tears would often burn his eyes and stream down his cheeks.

Why couldn't I have been born whole? he cried out from his soul. *The children all make fun of my twisted hand. They never let me play with them. My life is wasted and worthless. God has cursed me to live life crippled and helpless. Why has He been so cruel to me? I did nothing to deserve this punishment. It's not fair!* And the more he stirred his bitter, resentful thoughts, the faster Asa ran and the harder he cried. His only desire in life was to be whole. Surely God would hear and answer his prayer.

MIRIAM KNEW something was wrong. Now that puberty had arrived, her monthly period brought terrible cramps, pain, and days of bleeding. She talked with her mother about her unusually heavy bleeding. It wasn't normal: that's all her mother knew. Secretly she went to the village physician. Lycus was the Gentile doctor in her town of Hippos, part of the Decapolis.

Many Gentiles lived in this seaside town. Decades earlier, the Greeks from Alexander's army had come through the countryside and settled along the eastern side of the Sea of Galilee. Macedonian (or Greek) veterans from the wars planted themselves in the ten villages of the Decapolis.

Down through the generations after Alexander's conquest of the world, Jews who also desired to become more Hellenistic (Greek) in their ways had moved to the Greek towns hoping to learn the language and to become cultured in Greek ways. Greek was the language of trade and the arts throughout the Roman Empire. Jews hated all aspects of the culture of Rome, from her language of Latin to her multitude of gods. Many Jews had been put to death throughout the empire for refusing to pour libation offerings to Caesar as their king and god. Hellenized Jews read Plato, Socrates, and Philo, along with the Torah. They exercised naked like the Greeks in the gyms and spas and refused to be circumcised. Pharisees and Sadducees despised these renegade Jews and labeled them as pagans. But Miriam knew that a Jewish physician would immediately dismiss her as unclean and refuse to help her. Only the Gentile doctors schooled by the medical techniques of Hippocrates would help her.

Miriam had stored away coins for months. Some she found in the streets. Others were lying around the house unnoticed by her father or mother. Miriam's grandparents had moved to Hippos decades before to learn more about the Greek culture. Subsequently, her father had become wealthy by developing a lively trade in wool with the Greeks. So money was always around for Miriam to hide away. Besides, her father always gave his only child all that she asked. Whenever she entreated her father for a coin to buy sweets in the marketplace, he gladly gave her more than she needed.

Miriam kept her bleeding condition hidden from everyone. At age thirteen, she was now a woman and ready to be married, should some handsome man like Andrew ask for her hand in matrimony. But she knew that no Jew—no matter how Hellenized—would ever marry her if he knew her unclean condition. She felt so ashamed and dirty. Whenever the bleeding stopped for a few days, Miriam would hope and pray that this was the time of her healing. She prayed to Yahweh-Rapha (the God who heals) for help.

ASA RETURNED one evening from running and climbed the stairs at the side of his home up to the roof. Tears mingled with the sweat that poured from his body. He stripped down to his loin cloth and soaked in the pleasant evening breeze that cooled his body and began to soothe his spirit.

Asa gazed at the awesome canopy of stars that glistened across the cloudless sky. It was the new moon, so the stars seemed especially bright—no moonlight dimmed their radiance. *Why doesn't God heal me?* pondered Asa. He knew of no deep or secret sin in his life or his family. All were devout Jews worshipping God every Sabbath in the synagogue. Asa faithfully studied and memorized the Torah. How he loved the Word of God revealed to the great prophet Moses!

Some nights Asa dreamily imagined himself as the great Moses standing before Pharaoh and demanding, "Let my people go!" He saw himself lifting the rod of God over the Red Sea and the waters parting. He imagined himself climbing Mount Sinai and hearing the thunderous voice of God speak the commandments of the Law. But each fantasy abruptly ended the moment he caught sight of his twisted, withered hand.

The reality of his handicap dashed his dreams of importance and significance. Asa had no real hope of ever being *somebody*. His withered hand would always mark him as a reject from the blessings of God. He would have to settle for whatever menial work some gracious friend of his family might give him.

Since his father had died years before of some sudden sickness, Asa and his mother had lived in the house of her brother. Nothing belonged to Asa. No inheritance. No birthright. No hope. No dreams. No future. He had resigned himself to existing on the crumbs of life that might be thrown to him by his uncle. Asa's cousin, Isaac, continually laughed and mocked him. At best, Asa would always be the tag-along who played second fiddle to a cousin who regarded him as a nobody.

Asa searched the heavens each starlit night. Would Yahweh ever speak to him? Did God even know that he existed? Was it true that his withered hand was a sign of God's disfavor? As hopeless as he felt, Asa had a seed of expectancy deep in his spirit. The words of one of David's psalms stirred him beyond his circumstance: *The Lord is my shepherd, I shall not want.* Could the Lord really shepherd him? Would the Lord really take care of him? If the Lord so desired, would He heal Asa's hand?

As Asa longingly searched the heavens, stillness filled his soul. A salve of peace brought warmth and healing to his broken heart. Each night he climbed to the rooftop to commune with this mysterious God of Abraham, Isaac, and Jacob. Asa had heard the excited rabbis speak of a coming Anointed One who would free Israel from the Romans and set up God's kingdom on earth. Perhaps the promised Messiah would come soon. Perhaps in his kingdom, Asa would find the wholeness for which he so desperately longed.

MIRIAM GATHERED her coins together in a small coin bag and left by the back opening to their home. She wanted no one to see her. It was early morning, and her parents would think she had rushed to the well to chatter with the other young girls there. The well was the favorite spot in the village for young women to gossip and wishfully dream with one another about their future husbands. They excitedly whispered about the young men who noticed them from a distance. But Miriam rarely said anything at the well. She knew her malady would keep her from any hope of a betrothal. If only the Greek physician could find the cause and give her an herb or medicine that would heal her issue of blood!

So she rushed through the near empty streets of Hippos to the way called Magus and to the door of the physician called Lycus. She tapped on the door, and a young woman let her in. As Miriam was escorted through the house's atrium, she was awestruck. Climbing vines and blooming plants filled the sunlit room. A waterfall bubbled into a pool filled with fish. Never had she gazed upon such opulence. The young woman escorted her into a room filled with strange looking instruments and a multitude of vials containing curious concoctions of herbs, liquids, and balms.

A wiry, balding man in his late fifties greeted Miriam in broken Aramaic and had her sit on an ornate marble couch draped with finely woven wool cloths. Lycus carefully inquired about Miriam's health as he established a medical history for his new patient. Then he meticulously examined her while making notes on a parchment. Occasionally he would grunt and jot a note to himself. Finally, he sat back down on his stool. Miriam sat up and gazed intently into the doctor's compassionate eyes.

"I'm not sure what we have here," Lycus said softly. "We can try some special medicines that I have just received from Macedonia. Some doctors there have had success in stopping internal bleeding with them. But I cannot guarantee anything. Are you sure you want to try something new? It may be costly, and I'm not sure what side effects there may be."

"I will try anything," Miriam pleaded. "I have money," she offered, pulling her precious purse from under her robe.

"We will try. That's all I can promise," Lycus replied. "Perhaps something will work. If this medication doesn't stop the bleeding, there are some other exotic drugs we have from Egypt that may help. We will keep at this until something works. Who knows? Perhaps Zeus will smile upon us."

Inwardly, Miriam recoiled as the doctor invoked a pagan god. Yet, she knew that no Jewish doctor would ever help her. This was her only option. Hopefully, she poured all her coins into the doctor's outstretched hand. He then produced a small vial filled with yellow fluid.

"Take a sip of this twice a day whenever you are bleeding. Come back and see me in a month so that I can know if the medicine is working." Lycus then turned to leave the room and motioned for his young assistant to escort Miriam out.

Clutching the vial under her robe, Miriam hurried home with a heart brimming over with hope. *This might just work! And then I can hope for a husband and a normal life.* Slipping through the back door of her home, Miriam rushed to her room and uncorked the vial. *For a start, I will take more than a sip*, she reasoned. Gulping a mouthful of the bitter tasting potion, she replaced the cork and hid the vial under her bed.

Lying down for a few moments, she began to dream a dream she had buried for years. She saw herself caught up in the strong arms of handsome Andrew. Perhaps the day would soon come when her bleeding was stopped and she would be betrothed to him. What a day that would be! No more crumbs of conversation at the well. She too would have a man to talk about just like the others. The powerful drug began to course through her veins, making her drowsy. Like desert mirages disappearing as they are approached, her thoughts melted away into welcomed sleep.

ONE NIGHT as Asa pondered the starlit heavens from the rooftop, he noticed a bright star he had never seen before. In fact, the star was so bright it outshone every other heavenly orb. The moonless night seemed to enhance its brilliance. Moreover, the southern sky seemed to cast a beam of light earthward toward a spot south of where David's city was.

Could such a wonder in the heavens be a sign? Asa mused. He had just been reading the prophets over the last few months. Asa ventured less and less out of his home during the day. Watching the other teenagers play together and work at their father's trades was too painful for him. In fact, if his uncle had not been prosperous, Asa would have been destined to beg on the streets, since no one would ever hire a cripple like himself.

So Asa had resigned himself to studying the Torah (Law) and *Neviim* (Prophets). He had been fascinated by all the references in the Prophets to the coming King, called the Anointed One. Asa racked his brain to remember any prophecy that might connect this unusual star with the Messiah.

Suddenly, his breath rushed into his lungs with a gasp. Sweat poured from his palms. He began to tremble as he remembered the prophet from Judah, Micah, and his mysterious words,

> But thou, Bethlehem Ephrathah, though thou be little among the thousands of Judah, yet out of thee shall be come forth unto me that is to be ruler in Israel, whose goings forth have been from old, from everlasting.
>
> —Micah 5:2

The radiance from the star seemed to beam down directly over the area just south of Jerusalem. *It must be shining directly over Bethlehem!* thought Asa. Maybe this was the appointed time for Messiah. For centuries the Jews had settled for crumbs. First, the Macedonians had conquered them. After the overthrow of pagan ruler, Antiochus Epiphanes, with his desecration of the Temple, Israel had briefly enjoyed freedom until the iron fist of Rome enslaved them again. Most Jews prayed fervently for Messiah to come and break the yoke of bondage over God's people.

Could it be that Messiah even now was in Bethlehem as the prophet Micah had foretold? If so, would Asa ever see him? Such thoughts seemed too wondrous even to think. Each night for the next year he gazed at the remarkable star and prayed that someday he might meet the Messiah. Clutching his withered hand, he dared to hope that someday God might even heal him.

AS THE YEARS PASSED, Miriam found herself going from one doctor to another. Each one had a new remedy to try for healing her issue of blood. For months she would try the newest medication, only to be disappointed and even more desperate.

Both her father and mother had died, for Miriam had been a child born to them in their old age. Miriam had been the apple of their eyes and their consummate joy in life. Her entire inheritance was now being spent on one doctor after another.

Once she even traveled to Egypt upon hearing about a miracle cure for all kinds of maladies that was derived from poppy plants that grew along the Nile. While the medicine elevated her spirits, she had soon grown addicted to the drug and now constantly fed the dragon of addiction with all of her money and energy just to elevate her spirits.

But Miriam's issue of blood had grown worse over the years, and her desperation had begun to wane into despair. Almost out of money and hope, she languished in her home, rarely appearing in the streets except for her occasional trip to the market or the well. No one spoke to her any more. Her dreams of marriage had vanished long ago. Her daily existence was but an empty shell filled with broken dreams and shattered expectations. Only a miracle could restore her health and her faith in God. But no miracles were in sight, so she crawled through each day, barely existing on the crumbs of life.

AS ASA APPROACHED MID-LIFE, he filled his days with reading the Torah (Law), *Neviim* (Prophets), and the *Chetuvim* (Writings). With his good hand, he had learned to write impeccable Hebrew and worked as scribe for the rabbis.

Though unmarried, Asa felt his life was full with his work and love of reading the Scriptures.

Lately, Asa had been interested in the rumors about an itinerant preacher from Nazareth. This man, Yeshua, had been called by some a great prophet, and others were even bold enough to suggest that he might be the long-awaited Messiah. Rumors spread wildly among the Jewish leaders that this young upstart from Nazareth was even healing the sick and radically interpreting the Torah in strange and unusual ways.

But Asa dismissed the rumors. He knew that Messiah had to come from the lineage of David and be born in Bethlehem. *Nothing good can come out of the back country of Nazareth*, he thought.

Still, Asa was interested in the rumors. They put some life and interest into his monotonous days of writing new parchments of the Law for various synagogues throughout the region.

Late one Friday afternoon, Asa gathered up all his parchments and writing instruments in completion of another long week of writing. He stopped his work early on the sixth day of the week in preparation of Sabbath, which began promptly at sundown. As he washed and put on a fresh robe for the Sabbath service that evening, he once again stared at his withered hand. Asa remembered his childhood dreams of being healed someday and shuddered once again as he pictured in his mind those starlit nights when a new star blazed in the south over Bethlehem. *I wonder what that all meant*, he thought. *Just the fantasies of a boy*, he reasoned.

Life was better now. The crumbs that came his way through his work were certainly more satisfying than living off his cousin's income. He had been able to buy a small home for himself and his mother. Yes, they barely had enough to eat, but somehow they managed to survive without depending on the rest of the family. His independence meant more to him sometimes than even the hope of being healed. Asa had learned to make the best of his life, instead of aspiring to life's best.

> Asa had learned to make the best of his life, instead of aspiring to life's best.

In the cool evening air, Asa and his mother made their way toward the synagogue. Everyone in Capernaum was proud of this stately building that was unquestionably the best synagogue in the region. Of course, when they entered the building, his mother would sit in the back with the women while Asa would join the men who occupied the front and center seats of prominence and honor. Under the arm of his withered hand, he squeezed the parchment, quill, and ink he would use to write down what the rabbis said as they taught from the Torah that night.

His mother had already cleaned their small home and prepared the dinner candles for the Sabbath meal. Asa had gathered wildflowers in the field that afternoon as he did most Sabbaths in the spring to grace the table with color and sweet fragrances. Everything was prepared for his favorite meal of the week, which would be eaten joyfully after the evening Sabbath service.

As they entered the synagogue, Asa noticed a large crowd had gathered outside the building. This was unusual, because most of the town folks rarely attended the staid teachings in the synagogue. In fact, most of the Jews in the city had left regular teaching and worship to the devout Jews, while they only considered their Jewish faith at ceremonial times of the year.

Asa pushed through the crowd and went quickly to his place at a small table close to the front, while his mother found her saved place among the women. Pulling his *talit* (prayer shawl) over his head, Asa chanted the familiar opening *shema* for all the services, *Hear, O Israel: The Lord our God is one Lord.*

Much to his surprise, one of the synagogue's ruling rabbis did not proceed to the scroll for the reading of the Law. Instead, a strange man walked calmly to the front, took the scroll from out of its tabernacle, and turned to read the Law. Suddenly, Asa's heart began to pound the same way it had on the rooftop the night he first saw the star over Bethlehem. He began to tremble uncontrollably.

Attempting to pick up his quill and prepare to write, he dropped his pen and then embarrassingly knocked over his inkwell as he reached with his good hand to retrieve his quill. A few heads turned toward him to see what was causing the commotion, and Asa's face blushed with embarrassment. He felt the old hurt feelings from his childhood begin to rush to the surface . . . feelings of inadequacy, shame, and guilt for his withered hand. But his trembling would not stop, and his heart continued to pound.

As Asa sat back up and looked toward the podium in front of the room, the Galilean stranger was staring directly at him. His steady gaze penetrated Asa's soul. Never had his eyes met such an intense stare—a gaze that seemed to unmask his every pretense and expose his every thought. He couldn't take his eyes off the man. And then he knew. This must be Yeshua, the one everyone was talking about. This Nazarene had such an uncommon presence and authority that Asa felt that he and this prophet were the only two people in the crowded room.

Then Asa knew. This was the man who had been born in Bethlehem and whose star Asa had seen from the rooftop. He remembered the rumors that Jesus' parents had traveled to Bethlehem that year of the star because Caesar had ordered a rare census for taxing the Jews. This was the man who had been preaching in the countryside and drawing huge crowds. This was the man who spoke of God's kingdom coming now, and this was the man who healed all who touched him.

Asa's eyes remained glued to Jesus. Then he heard him speak: "Stand forth."

Asa looked around him. There was no one behind him: his table sat right up against the side wall of the synagogue. He desperately prayed that someone . . . anyone . . . would stand besides him. Yet, looking back into His eyes, Asa knew that the Galilean's words were meant only for him.

What could he want with me?, thought Asa. *He does not know me. I have no use for him. My life has been so simple as a scribe. Why can't I live an obscure existence and never be noticed again? If something happens to me today as a result of this Nazarene, then all the rulers of the synagogue will put me out. I will be an outcast once again. And I couldn't bear such a fate.*

Without another thought, Asa rose to his feet. For the first time in years, he felt self-conscious about his paralyzed hand. He awkwardly put his hand behind his back so that the stranger would not notice his deformity.

"Is it lawful to do good on the Sabbath days, or to do evil? To save life or to kill?" asked Jesus.

Asa burned with an inner fire he had never felt. Like molten gold flowing from a hot furnace, a river of fire began to flow from his shoulder down toward his withered hand. Every muscle in his left arm and hand started to tingle.

Throughout the synagogue, everyone kept absolutely silent. No one dared to answer this prophet from Nazareth. Jesus looked again directly at Asa. In that moment it seemed as though time stood still. The Law that Asa had loved and almost worshipped spun like a whirlwind in his head. All the answers he had been sure about from the prophets through the ages seemed to evaporate into thin air. This man spoke with such authority and power that Asa knew within his spirit that He was the promised Messiah.

A look of sadness filled Jesus' eyes as He looked around the room and perceived the hardness of everyone's hearts. They would not like what he was about to do. But this sign came from His Father, not from Himself. He never spoke or acted without His Father's command.

"Stretch forth your hand," Jesus commanded Asa.

Asa hesitated. Should he obey the stranger and risk

embarrassment or return to his seat and receive the approving looks of his colleagues? His whole reputation was at stake. If he obeyed this Jesus of Nazareth, he would be rejected by the synagogue rulers. Everything in his mind screamed, *Sit down! Be safe and stay secure in your position.*

But Asa's spirit had been in a dry season since childhood. All the writing and reading of the Scriptures had not satisfied his longing and thirsting for God's presence. Strangely, these few moments in the same room with Jesus had touched his heart like no other moment in his life. Without explanation, Asa simply knew that the Messiah had just addressed him, and now his eternity hung in the balance.

Asa looked at his withered hand. For a lifetime, he had felt nothing in it. It was a lifeless, worthless appendage that served no purpose. He remembered the childlike prayers he had cried on the rooftop asking God to heal him. Could God have really heard a child's prayers? Could this really be happening to him?

A sensation like fire shot through his arm. For a fleeting moment, Asa truly believed that his dead hand could move. Without another thought, he tried to open his twisted, clinched fist. He felt something! First, one finger and then another responded. Life seemed to flow into each muscle, tendon, and blood vessel. His hand began to burn like a raging fire. As he watched almost like a bystander, Asa saw his hand move and then stretch. He shook his fingers. He flexed his hand. Every muscle worked. Every fiber in his hand pulsed with power and life.

Like the air rushing out of a popped balloon, the entire crowd in the synagogue gasped with disbelief. Many of them had known Asa since birth. He had always been paralyzed in his left hand, never able to move even one finger. Now he stretched and moved every finger at will, and his hand returned to the suppleness of a newborn babe.

The angry rulers of the synagogue moved toward Jesus in order to force him out of the room. But mysteriously, he passed through them without one touching him. And Asa also moved, not toward his friends but toward this newfound friend. His spirit leapt within him with delight. Tears of joy filled Asa's face. His mother stood up and began climbing over people toward her son. At the top of her voice she shouted, "He's healed! My son is well! Jesus healed my son's hand! He must be Messiah!"

Like angry bouncers in a tavern, the whole body of Jews roughly pushed Asa and his mother from the room. But all Asa could do was stare at Yeshua. He had no desire to go anywhere but where He went. Without hesitation, Asa bid farewell to his mother and pushed through the crowd to follow Jesus. He had no thought of returning home. Every few seconds, Asa flexed his hand and looked down at it in amazement.

Jesus was walking a few yards ahead of him. A small group of men walked next to the prophet. And then others followed behind—some women and other people who seemed intent to be as close to Jesus as possible. That was now Asa's desire. He would follow this prophet wherever he went.

The lights of Capernaum faded in the distance as the small band of followers walked with Jesus down the dusty trail toward the seashore. Asa felt fully alive for the first time in his existence. Not only was his hand healed, but his inner being felt new and whole. Racing through Asa's mind were all the prophecies about Messiah he had faithfully copied as a scribe through the years. All of them fit. All of them now made sense. Here indeed was Messiah. And Asa had just been healed by His word. The only name that Asa could think to call him was *Master*.

Finally his lips uttered the word on his heart, "Master." It was only a whisper from the back of the crowd, but Jesus stopped. He turned and met Asa's eyes. Tears of gratitude streamed down Asa's face. He fell to his knees and worshipped from his heart as he never had before. As he lifted his tear-streaked face, Asa gazed into the Master's face, lit not only by the torches but also by a glow that Asa had never seen on any other face. Silently, speaking heart-to-heart as only friends can, Jesus nodded and motioned for Asa to rise and to continue to follow him. As Jesus turned and continued down the path, Asa stood up and followed his Messiah.

Never again would Asa grab for a meager existence. Now

he knew life Himself. Now, he knew that in Jesus, there would be *No More Crumbs!*

THE SUN FLOODED into Miriam's tiny room. The familiar stream of blood issued from her body and pooled on the bed beneath her. She quietly gathered the unclean rags and put them in a basket that she would carry to the garbage heap outside of town and burn at sunset.

This was the day she went to the market to shop for some meager supplies that would barely sustain her body. She had grown weaker each month and was as pale as the snow on Mount Hermon.

As she made her way to the market, carrying a small basket for her paltry goods, Miriam stumbled headlong into a large crowd, making it impossible to reach her destination. "What's happening?" she asked the nearest woman.

"Haven't you heard?" replied the surprised woman. "The Prophet from Nazareth is walking through our town. Can you imagine it? And everyone wants to catch a glimpse of Him."

"What's so special about him? Prophets come and go," Miriam grouched.

"They call this one Jesus. Some say He is the Messiah. Besides, everywhere He goes, people are healed by simply touching him."

Suddenly Miriam was very interested. *Healed!* she thought excitedly. *No, not me, I'm just an unclean woman. If anyone saw me even come close to him they would stone me to death. He would never touch an unclean woman with an issue of blood.*

Without warning, the crowd started moving toward her. Miriam was being pushed back by the crush of bodies rushing toward her. Before she knew it, Miriam had fallen to her knees and was crawling on the ground, frantically searching for her dropped basket.

The crowd stopped, and so did she. *This is my chance,* she thought. *No one will notice if I crawl through the crowd toward this man. He can't reject me. He won't even see me. And if I can just touch the hem of his robe, perhaps I will be healed. I have nothing to lose. All my money and medicine is gone. No doctor has ever been able to help me. And if they discover me and stone me, so what. I would rather die than go on living like this.*

Miriam crawled through the crowd toward a voice that had begun teaching. "The well have no need of a physician, but I have come to heal the sick," the prophet said. As He continued to speak, Miriam followed the sound of His voice until it was immediately above her. Dust choked her lungs. Every muscle ached as she used her last reserve of strength to reach out and touch the Prophet's robe.

Suddenly, everything stopped. Miriam felt power surge through her. It was unlike anything she had ever known. Immediately, the ever-flowing stream of blood that issued from her womb dried up. She was healed!

That same voice she had heard a moment earlier now spoke directly to her. "Who touched me?" Jesus asked.

"Everyone has been touching you," protested the men around him. "The whole crowd has been pushing in on you."

"No, someone touched the hem of my robe, and power flowed out of me to her." By this time the crowd had parted, and Miriam fell prostrate in front of Jesus. Trembling out of control and sobbing floods of tears, she told him all the truth of her life's story. All the doctors . . . all the money . . . all the medicine she had used were all for naught. He had been her last hope. And now she was whole.

As she sobbed her thanks, Jesus quietly spoke to her, "Daughter, your faith has made you whole. Go in peace, and be healed of your affliction."

Jesus turned and proceeded toward Jarius' house, where his daughter lay dead. The crowd carefully sidestepped the sobbing Miriam, whose tears now flowed from joy, not sorrow.

Gingerly, a man with two strong hands lifted her up to her feet. She gazed into the kind face of a stranger whose eyes were literally dancing with joy. "Daughter, what is your name, and where do you live?" he asked.

"I am Miriam," she replied. "And my home is just down the street."

"I will walk you there and help you home," he replied.

As they walked toward her house, Miriam stopped and turned back toward the crowd winding their way through the narrow streets toward Jarius' house.

"Is He the One?" she asked hopefully.

"Yes, He is the Anointed One. I follow Him wherever he goes."

"Can I also follow Him? I have nothing left at home to go back to. Are women allowed to follow?" Miriam inquired with hesitant hope in her voice.

"Yes," he answered. "Many women follow him. Mary, Martha, and a former prostitute named Magdalene all faithfully follow him. You can join them on the road."

Miriam turned her back on the home that had been her prison for years. New strength filled her body. Songs of joy played in her spirit. Her eyes burned with love for this Jesus, the Messiah.

As they walked, Miriam glanced at the man's hand that firmly held hers. It looked so strong, and the skin that covered it looked almost like a baby's.

"And what is your name?" she asked.

"I am Asa," he smiled.

"And why do you follow him?"

"Like you, he healed me. The hand that holds yours was made new by Jesus," Asa testified.

Both Asa and Miriam followed the man from Nazareth through the winding streets. Not knowing all that would lie ahead, of one fact they were both sure. Their dry seasons had been left behind. The Jesus they now followed had spoken the same truth to their hearts:

No More Crumbs!

8

On the Edge of Your Breakthrough

A S THE WOMAN with an issue of blood crawled through the crowd on her hands and knees reaching out to touch the hem of the Master's robe, she was on the edge of her breakthrough (Mark 5).

As the man with the withered hand heard the Master say, "Stretch forth thy hand," that man was on the edge of his breakthrough (Mark 3).

As the prodigal son shoveled pig slop and searched for food, he came to his senses, and in that moment he was on the edge of his breakthrough (Luke 15).

When the sower went forth to sow and then slept day and

night while first the blade, then the ear, and finally the full grain in the ear burst out, he stood on the breakthrough of his harvest (Mark 4).

When Mephibosheth left Lo-debar and entered the royal dining room spread with a banquet just in his honor, he knew that he had arrived at the edge of his breakthrough (2 Sam. 9).

> **Before the breakthrough comes the vision of what God can and will do if you will act in faith.**

Before the breakthrough comes the vision of what God can and will do if you will act in faith. Notice this: it's not vision we lack but resolve.

Breaking through to no more crumbs requires much of us. God has done his part. He has issued the invitation, *Come to My table. Eat of my flesh. Drink of my blood. Dwell in me and I will dwell in you* (John 6).

All the elements needed for a breakthrough have been provided by God for you. The breakthrough for your harvest is here. The breakthrough for your healing is here. The breakthrough for your prospering is here. The breakthrough for your inheritance is here. But will you leave Lo-debar with the resolve and perseverance to break through every obstacle and stronghold in order to realize God's vision for you? God's vision is **No More Crumbs!** Will you break through?

PEACE:
THE BREAKTHROUGH OF RECONCILIATION

RECONCILIATION requires repentance; repentance requires recognition. Before Mephibosheth could leave Lo-debar, he had to recognize two essential truths:

- God's vision for him could not be realized in Lo-debar.

- To claim his inheritance he had to leave Lo-debar and be reconciled to the king.

Recognize your need for God.

In recognizing that his present circumstances were not God's vision for him, Mephibosheth had a breakthrough. Breakthroughs always start when we recognize that we cannot stay where we are. Lo-debar is where you are—lack, stagnation, deprivation, sickness, depression, despair, and hopelessness. When you make friends with those stuck in Lo-debar, you lose your desire to get out, to break through.

Paul writes in 2 Corinthians 5:17, "Therefore, *if* any man be in Christ, he is a new creature; old things are passed away; behold, all things are become new" (italics mine). So what components go into that *if?* Simply these:

- *If* we recognize that we are living in the old and need a new life in Christ.

- *If* we recognize our desire to going on with God instead of holding back.

- *If* we recognize that fear and despair are the only friends we have in Lo-debar.

- *If* we determine to have the resolve to follow God's vision and leave our own selfish, desolate dreams behind.

"Where there is no vision, the people perish; but he that keepeth the law, happy is he" (Prov. 29:18). Integral to breakthrough is obedience to God's vision. When God gives a vision, we must be ready and willing to obey. The fruit of obedience is rooted in the unquenchable desire for God. "As the deer panteth after the water brooks, so panteth my soul after thee, O God. My soul thirsteth for God, for the living God" (Ps. 42:1–2a).

When God gives a vision, we must be ready and willing to obey.

Repent of past sin.

To repent means to turn away from sin and to move obediently toward God. In order to leave the pig pen, the prodigal son had to repent. "Father, I have sinned against heaven, and before thee" (Luke 15:18).

Whatever in the past has kept us from breaking through to God must be renounced and left behind. For Mephibosheth there was no turning back to Lo-debar. For the sower, there is no turning back once the seed is sown. The harvest will come! For the prodigal son there's no turning back to the pigpen. For the man with a withered hand and the woman with an issue of blood, there's no turning back to infirmity.

Your breakthrough lies on the other side of your complacency. You will never have a breakthrough if you sit around doing nothing and expecting God to do everything. The truth is that God has already done all He needs to do. His Son died on the cross, saving you from sin and healing you by His stripes. God has already provided your inheritance for abundant life now and eternal life forever. He has set before you a vision of doing even greater things than Christ did (John 14:12). The greatest thing restraining you is complacency.

> Your breakthrough lies on the other side of your complacency.

In complacency you trade in your armor of God for a harmless garment of comfort.

Complacent and comfortable, you become a sick eaglet never mounting up on eagle's wings. As a spent pilgrim, you give up the journey and sit by the wayside hoping to get some small pleasure from sniffing the wilted flowers of past successes. Your convictions have been neutralized, and your desire to do great and mighty exploits for the Lord has been reduced to a monotonous recital of what the Lord has done, not who He is and what He will do. So your spiritual growth is stunted.

—A.W. Tozer

The Spirit of God is quenched. The fire that waxed in your bones has grown lukewarm, and the gifts of the Spirit that once stirred within you lay dormant.

What must you do? Repent! (Acts 2:38; 2 Cor. 7:9–10). Turn away from the sin of lazy comfort and languishing in past memories. Refuse to pick up old sin, offenses, and failures.

Be reconciled to God.

Come home to the Father. Make peace with God. "Therefore, being justified by faith, we have peace with God through our Lord Jesus Christ. For if, when we were enemies, we were reconciled to God by the death of his Son, much more, being reconciled, we shall be saved by his life" (Rom. 5:1, 10).

Don't expect a breakthrough until you first have a relationship with God.

Reconciliation is making peace with God. Mephibosheth had to make peace with the king. The prodigal son rushed home to be reconciled with his father. We can never claim God's vision and plan for our lives until we first have an intimate, personal relationship with Him through

Christ. Don't expect a breakthrough until you first have a relationship with God.

POSITION: RESTORATION TO ROYALTY

THE FIRST STEP to no more crumbs is peace that brings reconciliation. The next step is position. God wants to restore you to your rightful position in the Kingdom of God. What is that position?

Royalty is your position.

> But ye are a chosen generation, a royal priesthood, an holy nation, a people of his own, that ye should show forth the praises of him who hath called you out of darkness into his marvelous light; Who in time past were not a people but are now the people of God; who had not obtained mercy but now have obtained mercy.
>
> —1 Peter 2:9–10

In each story from biblical history, we uncovered how each person was restored to his or her rightful position in God's kingdom.

Mephibosheth took his position at the king's table. The prodigal son returned home to a feast thrown by his father to rejoice over his homecoming. The man with the withered hand and the woman with the issue of blood both were restored to a position of health and wholeness.

Not only are we priests and kings—a holy nation—we are

also friends with Christ. Jesus tells us, "Henceforth I call you not servants; for the servant knoweth not what his lord doeth: but I have called you friends; for all things that I have heard of my Father I have made known unto you" (John 15:15). We are blood-bought and Holy Ghost-filled. That makes us blood brothers and sisters with Jesus Christ. He sealed the covenant of our restoration with His blood just as blood covenants of the ancient world were sealed. We are in the family of the King. We are princes of the King of Kings and lords under subjection to the Lord of Lords.

Your rightful position is in the heavenlies in Christ. "And hath raised us up together, and made us sit together in heavenly places in Christ Jesus" (Eph. 2:6). You are no longer under the table sweeping for crumbs. You are at the table of Christ drinking from His cup and eating of His bread. You have left Lo-debar and the far country with its pig sties. Jesus has set for you a position of honor at His table. He has restored you completely and brought you from shame to honor, guilt to forgiveness, lack to abundance, and from sickness to health.

Restoration has been accomplished.

Your inheritance has been restored. Your family has been reunited. Your future is secure. And your position has been firmly established.

When an antique furniture dealer buys an old table at a garage sale, no one understands its value. The veneer is chipped. The finish is worn. The legs may be broken and the supports may be wobbly, but the dealer knows its intrinsic value. He takes the old table back to his shop and begins to patiently restore it. The old finish is removed, and the table is freshly stained. The veneer, legs, and supports are repaired. Old things are passing away. Everything about the table is becoming new (2 Cor. 5:17). What was a worthless piece of junk at the garage sale now takes the honored place in the show window of the dealer's shop. Everyone who passes by marvels at the fine, restored piece of furniture. Its value has been restored. The table's beauty, usefulness and worth have all been restored by the master craftsman.

Now the time has come to lay down our tambourines of praise and pick up our weapons of attack.

So it is with our lives. We are old, worn, useless, and worthless. Sin has aged us and ruined our shine and luster. Our only worth is to be cast into the fire and used for kindling. But Jesus sees through our old nature and values us. He buys us from the junk heap and restores our image and worth. We become brand new through Him, and His restoration gives us an honored position at His table. With praise and joy, we exclaim with David, "He restoreth my soul" (Ps. 23:3).

PROVISION:
RENEWING OUR ATTACK

NOW THE TIME HAS COME to lay down our tambourines of praise and pick up our weapons of attack. God has given us the word of restoration. He has returned what the enemy has stolen and the locusts have eaten. Now God wants us to attack the giants and possess the land.

There came a time in Mephibosheth's life when he had to take action to possess the inheritance that belonged to him. The prodigal son had to put on the robe and ring in order to walk in the provision of his father. The man with the paralyzed hand had to stretch forth his hand in order to receive his healing. The woman with the issue of blood had to determine to crawl through the crowd, reach out and touch the hem of Jesus' robe before she could be healed. And the sower had to prepare the land and sow the seed before he could reap a harvest.

"But Pastor Parsley," you may protest. "I'm just waiting on God. Some day my ship will come in, or maybe I'll win the sweepstakes or the lottery. Then I will claim my provision from God. Then I will mount the attack."

Please understand that God's provision has already been given to us through the cross and resurrection of Jesus Christ. His provision of abundant life is for now. His provision of eternal life is our everlasting inheritance. So what are you waiting for? Attack!

Attack your giants.

Yes, there are giants you may have to kill before you attack. The giants you must slay are:

- *Unbelief.* Unbelief is guilty of infanticide—murdering many infant petitions. Thousands of prayers to attack and bring down the enemy have been strangled in their infancy by unbelief.

- *Fear.* Mephibosheth, the prodigal son, the man with the withered hand, and the woman with the issue of blood all had become accustomed to Lo-debar. They could have simply stayed in the wilderness of their lack and the pain of their affliction. At least they knew what was in Lo-debar, but to claim God's provision and attack the enemy was moving into unknown territory. The fear of the known present is sometimes more appealing to us than the unknown battles of the future.

But remember, the battle that you face is not about your past. Jesus has forgiven and cleansed your past. The battle you now fight is about your future, and your children's future and their children's future. You overcome the fear not just for your sake but for the sake of future generations who will receive the promise of God's inheritance from you. Will you have any conquered territory to bequeath them?

> You overcome the fear not just for your sake but for the sake of future generations who will receive the promise of God's inheritance from you.

- *Opinions of men.* Remember when Israel was in the wilderness about to cross over into the Promised Land that God had provided? The nation allowed the opinions of ten fearful men to count more than the courage and boldness of two righteous men—Caleb and Joshua. They advised that the land could be taken and the giants defeated. No longer would Israel have to settle for just crumbs in the wilderness. They could obtain the provision and possess the land flowing with milk and honey. But the people listened to the naysayers— ten men who memories are forgotten and legacies lost because they would not attack the giants and possess the land. Are you listening to God or men? Do you follow God's ideas or man's ideas? Are you sitting at the table or still crawling around under it?

- *Discouragement.* "David encouraged himself in the Lord" (1 Sam. 30:6). Failing at times doesn't make you a failure. A baseball all-star may fail two out of three times in getting a hit. But getting one hit out of three makes him a success, not a failure! One bad day doesn't negate the previous three or four good days in the Lord. Attack! Don't let a setback cause you to retreat. Press on to the high calling of Christ.

- *Complacency.* Another word for complacency is laziness (Heb. 6:2). Proverbs tells us to consider the industry of the ant. Paul warns us that those who do not work should not eat. God has already acted. Jesus died for you. Jesus rose from the dead for you. Jesus sent the

Holy Spirit to baptize you with power. The ball is in your court. The inheritance is there for you to claim and the land for you to possess.

These are the giants you must slay in order to take up God's provision and renew your attack. Remember that it is not a vision that we lack, but the resolve to leave our comfort zones in Lo-debar and to move out with God.

You have mighty weapons with which to attack. Here are just a few:

- *The Word of God.* Before the Israelites crossed the Jordan, God commanded them to meditate on the Law day and night (Joshua 1:8). In order to attack the enemy and possess the provision God had given Israel, God's people needed the sword of the Spirit— God's Word (Eph. 6:17).

- *Prayer.* Be persistent in prayer (Luke 18:1–8) and diligently seek the Lord (Heb. 11:6). As we pray through to God's vision of provision, the vision is clear, the virtue is mighty, and the victory is assured. God has given us the weapon of prayer to pull down the enemy's strongholds and possess the land. The whole life of the believer is prayer—every act, thought, word, and wish. Our types of prayer weapons include:

  1. Praying with the authority to bind and loose (Matt. 16:19).

2. Praying in agreement (Matt. 18:19).

3. Praying to petition God (Mark 11:22–24).

4. Praying with thanksgiving and praise (2 Chr. 20).

5. Praying to commit, dedicate, and consecrate (Phil. 4:6–7).

6. Praying in intercession (Rom. 8:26).

7. Praying in the Spirit; building up ourselves in the Holy Spirit (1 Cor. 14; Jude 20).

- *Faith.* In knowing God there is an explosion of faith (Heb. 11). By faith the paralyzed man stretched for his hand and was healed. By faith the woman with the issue of blood reached out, touched the hem of Jesus' garment, and was healed. By faith the sower goes out to sow and receives a harvest. By faith Mephibosheth trusted the word of David's servant, came to the palace, and received the provision of the king. "And all things, whatever ye shall ask in prayer, believing, ye shall receive" (Matt. 21:22).

- *The gifts of the Holy Spirit.* Stir up the gift in you (2 Tim. 1:6). You would collapse from sheer external pressure were there not a counter pressure within you sufficiently great enough to push back (1 John 4:4). The same Spirit who raised Jesus from the dead now dwells in you (Rom. 8). So let the Spirit within you flow out of you as fountains of living water ministering God's provision.

- *The assembling of saints together.* The body of Christ comes together for worship, work, edification, ministry, and praise (Heb. 10:25). We must assemble as the body of Christ to be equipped for His work (Eph. 4:12). We are the living stones of the building of God (1 Pet. 2:5). The Church (*ecclesia*) has been called out of darkness and the world to walk in His glorious light, so that the world might see and witness the Light of Christ. We are members of one body with each member needed and important (1 Cor. 12) for the battle that we fight. Satan's plan is to isolate and destroy sheep. We are joined together as the Church, and built together on the rock of Christ the gates of hell cannot stand against us (Matt. 16:18).

- *Worship and praise.* As the people marched around the walls of Jericho shouting their praises and worshipping God, the walls came down (Josh. 6). The same is true for you. The walls of the enemy separating you from God's provision will come tumbling down as you praise Him for what He has already provided for you. You may not see the provision yet, but trust His Word and praise Him. We walk by faith and not by sight (2 Cor. 5:7). Worship and praise Him for what He has done, is doing, and will do (Ps. 103).

- *Ministering good works to others in Jesus' name.* Take the battle to the enemy. Invade his territory. Feed the hungry, clothe the naked, visit the lonely and imprisoned, and minister to the sick as unto Jesus (Matt. 25).

The anointing of God's Spirit is upon you to preach good news in the enemy's camp; to bind up the broken-hearted; to proclaim liberty to the captives; and to open up the prisons for those who are bound (Isa. 61:1). Take the weapon of your good works and march right into the enemy's camp, boldly proclaiming Jesus' name. Set the captives free. Bring God glory and take back what the enemy has stolen. "Let your light so shine before men, that they may see your good works, and glorify your Father, who is in heaven" (Matt. 6:16).

PRIVILEGE:
PERPETUAL HARVEST

> The fields are ripe to harvest! Pray for workers in the harvest.

TIME IS ACCELERATING. The harvest immediately follows the sowing. Reaping and sowing come together in the same season. The promised harvest is upon us. For generations, men like William Seymore, Oral Roberts, Smith Wigglesworth, and Lester Sumerall have been sowing. Both their harvest and the harvest resulting from our sowing is ready in the fields. We cannot let it spoil there.

The outpouring of God's Spirit upon our generation is beginning to flow from the throne of God through us and into our world. The river of God brings His abundant harvest. At first in Ezekiel 47:3, the river was only ankle deep. The spiritual walk of God's people was touched, but much in their lives needed refreshing. "Repent, therefore, and be converted, that your sins may be blotted out, when the times of refreshing shall come from the presence of God" (Acts 3:19). Those times of refreshing are flowing through us, but there is more!

Then the river of God flows up to our knees (Ezek. 47:4). Our prayer lives are beginning to explode with authority and intercession. God's hand is being moved by our prayers (Acts 10:1–4). We are seeking corporate prayer by the body of Christ to shake our churches out of their complacency; to shake our preachers out of laziness and man's traditions; to shake God's people bringing them to their knees in prayer and intercession; and to shake our communities, bringing a new hunger and thirst for God throughout our land. The fields are ripe to harvest! Pray for workers in the harvest.

Then the river of God flows waist deep (Ezek. 47:4) inspiring us to gird up our loins, to run the race with patience, to fix our eyes on Jesus, and to minister in His name with signs and wonders.

We have witnessed the river touching our ankles, our knees, and our waists. But now there is more. The river is so deep and wide that we cannot leave anything in our lives untouched by God's Spirit. We must swim in the river (Ezek. 47:5). We are immersed and baptized by His Spirit. The river of God will produce a perpetual harvest resulting in a corporate explosion of:

Leadership.

We are sowing into the lives of Christians around the

world to disciple and grow up leaders in the body of Christ for the fivefold offices of the church: pastors, evangelists, teachers, preachers, and apostles (Eph. 4).

Unity.

In one accord, Spirit-filled and baptized believers are coming together in the body of Christ with all parts and members working as one body to the glory of God (Ps. 133; 1 Cor. 12; Eph. 4).

Evangelism.

The fields are ready for the harvest, and we must pray in the workers (Matt. 9:37–38). Harvest time is a season of marked growth in grace and discipleship. It's time to take the sickle and work the harvest. The plowman is overtaking the reaper as the sowing and reaping come in the same season.

> Behold, the days come, saith the Lord, that the plowman shall overtake the reaper, and the treader of grapes him that soweth seed; and the mountains shall drop sweet wine, and all the hills shall melt.
>
> —Amos 9:13

Families being reclaimed.

The hearts of the fathers are being turned to the children. In this season of no more crumbs, families will be restored and their wholeness will herald the return of Jesus' (Mal. 4:5–6).

Now is the time for you to leave Lo-debar. Your dry season is over.

- Come out from under the table, gathering a meager meal of crumbs.

- Sit in your royal position at the King's table.

- Take back and possess the land the enemy has stolen.

- Reap the harvest that the locusts can no longer devour.

- Watch and pray for the tiny cloud only the size of a man's hand that will bring the refreshing rain of God onto the parched fields of your life.

- Sow in your famine so that you might reap a bountiful harvest.

- Enter into the banquet feast your Father has spread for you.

- Touch the hem of the Master's garment and be healed.

- Stretch forth your hand and be made whole.

- Start swimming in the river of God. The dam is breaking and your breakthrough is at hand.

Declare boldly in Jesus' name:

No More Crumbs!

Conclusion

Come to His Table

THERE WAS A CERTAIN RICH MAN, who was clothed in purple and fine linen, and fared sumptuously every day. And there was a certain beggar, named Lazarus, who was laid at his gate, full of sores. And desiring to be fed with the crumbs which fell from the rich man's table; moreover, the dogs came and licked his sores. And it came to pass, that the beggar died, and was carried by the angels into Abraham's bosom: the rich man also died, and was buried; And in hell he lift up his eyes, being in torments, and seeth Abraham afar off, and Lazarus in his bosom.

And he cried and said, Father Abraham, have mercy on me, and send Lazarus, that he may dip the tip of his finger in water, and cool my tongue; for I am tormented in this flame. But Abraham said, Son, remember that thou in thy lifetime receivest thy good things, and likewise Lazarus evil things: but now he is comforted, and thou art tormented. And beside all this, between us and you there is a great gulf fixed: so that they which would pass from hence to you cannot; neither can they pass to us, that would come from thence. Then he said, I pray thee therefore, father, that thou wouldest send him to my father's house: For I have five brethren; that he may testify unto them, lest they also come into this place of torment.

Abraham saith unto him, They have Moses and the prophets; let them hear them. And he said, Nay, father Abraham: but if one went unto them from the dead, they will repent. And he said unto him, If they hear not Moses and the prophets, neither will they be persuaded, though one rose from the dead.

—Luke 16:19–31

As I read this text, I actually see two beggars here, not one. Lazarus begs in time that a morsel of bread from the rich man's table may fill the cavernous void of his empty and tormented stomach, while he lay at the gate and suffered from a multitude of sores covering his body. All he wanted from life were the crumbs that fell from the rich man's table.

But there's another beggar here, the rich man, who does not beg in time but begs in eternity. After both men die, Lazarus goes to Abraham's bosom while the rich man finds himself in hell. Looking across the abyss, the rich man sees Lazarus and begs for a drop of water from his hand to cool the rich man's tongue in hell. But Lazarus cannot cross the abyss, so the rich man begs for Lazarus to return to earth and warn his father's household about the torment that awaits them if they do not repent.

One beggar begged in time and the other begged in eternity. We each face this choice: Will we beg for God's mercy in this life and be restored to the Father's table, or will we wait until it's too late? If we do not repent in time, then the banquet that Jesus has spread for His bride will not be ours to taste. The rich man ended up begging for all eternity and never being satisfied.

> We each face this choice: Will we beg for God's mercy in this life and be restored to the Father's table, or will we wait until it's too late?

One of London's most notorious gangsters in all of its history was Mr. Peace. He pillaged homes, raped women, and murdered children until finally the law caught him and sentenced him to death by hanging. As he walked out of his cell toward the gallows, Mr. Peace met a preacher reading the Bible aloud to him. He jerked the preacher up by the nape of his neck and screamed, "Preacher, do you believe that?"

The preacher sputtered, "Believe what?"

"Do you believe in hell?" asked the condemned man. "Do you believe in a place of eternal incarceration? I've been incarcerated in these walls, but do you believe in a place where I can be locked up and never released throughout the endless ages of eternity? Do you believe in a place called hell, Preacher?"

"Well, yes, I suppose I do," replied the preacher.

Throwing the preacher down to the ground, Mr. Peace disdainfully retorted, "That's the most pathetic statement I have ever heard. For if I believed in your God and a place you so casually refer to as hell—a place of eternal torment and everlasting fire—though the road from Hoe in the north of England to Liverpool in the south be paved with broken and jagged glass, upon my hands and knees would I crawl until my limbs were nothing more than bloody stumps if, perchance at the end of the road, there would be some poor person that I could tell and give the message that would cause him to escape eternity in such a wretched place!"

My final plea with you is twofold. If you are a beggar in eternity without a knowledge of the Lord Jesus Christ, then now is the time for your salvation. Before you can claim your rightful inheritance as a child of God, you must repent of your sin and confess Jesus Christ as your Lord and Savior. Fall to your knees this moment and beg the Father just as the prodigal son did:

Father, I have sinned against heaven and You. I repent of my sins and receive the shed blood of Jesus to cleanse me from sin. I thank You, Jesus, for saving me and giving me the gift of Your Holy Spirit. Baptize and fill me with Your Spirit. I surrender my life to You and I will follow You for eternity. Amen.

Perhaps you are like Lazarus, a beggar in time. Saved but powerless, hopeless, and helpless in life—simply waiting for crumbs to fall from someone else's table. You have resigned yourself to be a saint crawling around in a wilderness, hoping to find a morsel of food or cup of water left behind by someone else. You cry and complain that life is hard and that serving Christ has left you destitute.

Get up off your hands and knees. Come out from under the table. There is an inheritance already won for you by Christ at Calvary. Stop acting like a slave and begin to put on the robes of royalty and the ring of authority. Come out of your pigpen and run headlong into the arms of your Father. He's waiting for you.

> Stop acting like a slave and begin to put on the robes of royalty and the ring of authority.

Too long you have wallowed in the mud of financial debt, marriage problems, parental crises, and strongholds at every turn. You are a saint, but you have chosen to dig in the unholy garbage of the world, looking for crumbs that will not satisfy. You are royalty, but you are wearing the worn, torn garments of a past still clinging to you.

- When will you leave the Lo-debar of your misery and self-pity?

- When will you begin to watch and pray for the rain

that is coming from God upon your dry season?

- When you will stop eating your pitiful handful of seed and sow it into a harvest of abundance?

- When will you stop running to every worldly remedy for your affliction and claim your healing by the stripes of Jesus?

- When will you cease your excuses for inactivity because of your withered handicap and stretch forth your hand to grasp His abilities, which meet all your inabilities?

- When will you come and take your seat at His table?

The Father has spread the table for you. The Son who came to serve you has come to bring you into the great feast prepared by the King for His royal children. Jesus simply takes bread and breaks it, saying, "Take, eat; this is my body." He takes the cup and hands it to you saying, "Drink ye all of it; For this is my blood of the new testament, which is shed for many for the remission of sins" (Matt. 26:26–28).

Do not remain in Lo-debar. Stretch forth your hand and take hold of your inheritance:

- His *peace* of reconciliation between you and the Father will flood your soul.

- Your *position* at His table will be restored.

- Your ***provision*** for daily bread is there, as is the power to renew your attack on the enemy and take back what he has stolen and the locusts have eaten.

- Your ***perpetual privilege*** to reap a ***promised harvest*** has been established. When you sow you will reap. The plowman will overtake the sower and you will see an abundant harvest of the lost. Your family will be restored. Your lost relatives and friends will be saved. You will be blessed to be a blessing.

Have you not heard? The Lord, your shepherd, has prepared a table before you in the presence of your enemies. He has anointed your head with the oil of His Spirit and power. He overflows your cup with living water that flows from the river of God. Goodness and mercy will follow you all the days of your life, and your dwelling place will be in His house forever!

Come to His table and boldly declare in Jesus' name:

No More Crumbs!

ABOUT THE AUTHOR

ROD PARSLEY began his ministry as an energetic nineteen-year-old in the backyard of his parents' Ohio home. The fresh, "old-time gospel" approach of Parsley's delivery immediately attracted a hungry, God-seeking audience. From the seventeen people who attended Parsley's first 1977 backyard meeting, the crowds rapidly grew.

Today, as the pastor of Columbus, Ohio's 5,200-seat World Harvest Church, Parsley oversees World Harvest's Christian Academy; World Harvest Bible College; Bridge of Hope missions and outreach; and "Breakthrough," World Harvest Church's daily and weekly television broadcast. Parsley's message to "raise the standard" of spiritual intensity, moral integrity, and physical purity not only extends across America but spans the globe, reaching throughout Canada and to nearly 150 nations via television and shortwave radio.

Thousands in arenas across the country and around the world can experience the saving, healing, delivering message of Jesus Christ as Parsley calls people back to Bible basics.

Rod Parsley currently resides in Pickerington, Ohio, with his wife, Joni, and their two children, Ashton and Austin.

OTHER BOOKS BY
ROD PARSLEY

Backside of Calvary
Breakthrough Quotes
The Commanded Blessing
Free at Last
God's Answer to Insufficient Funds
Holiness: Living Leaven Free
My Promise Is the Palace
No Dry Season
Repairers of the Breach
Serious Survival Strategies
Ten Golden Keys to Your Abundance
Tribulation to Triumph

For information about "Breakthrough" or
World Harvest Church or to receive a product list
of the many books and audio and videotapes
by Rod Parsley write or call:

"Breakthrough"
P.O. Box 32932
Columbus, Ohio 43232-0932
614-837-1990

For information about World Harvest Bible College,
write or call:

World Harvest Bible College
P.O. Box 32901
Columbus, Ohio 43232-0901
614-837-4088

If you need prayer, the "Breakthrough" prayer line is open
twenty-four hours a day, seven days a week.
614-837-3232